# BONDING

## RELATIONSHIPS
## IN THE
## IMAGE OF GOD

# Donald M. Joy, Ph.D.

**WORD BOOKS**
PUBLISHER
WACO, TEXAS

A DIVISION OF
WORD, INCORPORATED

BONDING: Relationships in the Image of God

Copyright © 1985 by Donald M. Joy

**Library of Congress Cataloging in Publication Data**

Joy, Donald M. (Donald Marvin), 1928—
  Bonding: relationships in the image of God.

  Bibliography: p.
  Includes index.
  1. Christian life—Methodist authors. 2. Interpersonal relations—Religious aspects—Christianity. 3. Intimacy (Psychology)
I. Title.
BV4501.2.J678  1985        248.4      84-27121
ISBN 0-8499-0440-4
ISBN 0-8499-3076-6 (TP)

*Printed in the United States of America*

7898 FG 987654321

FOR
*John and Julie*
*Mike and Dorian*
our sons and the brides
of their youth.
We celebrate their early wisdom
and embrace their friendship.
We applaud the smooth transitions
from childhood, to adolescence,
to marriage and parenthood.
We find fulfillment in our grandchildren:
a "quiver full of them"!
*Jason Donald Elwyn Joy*
*Heather Nicole Joy*
*Jami Maree Joy*
*Lesli Danielle Joy*
*Jordan Michael Joy*
*Justin Michael Brooks Joy*

The coat of arms for the HOUSE OF JOY consists of these:
Three fleur de lis
Above a silver chevron
Roofing a rampant lion.

Let the fleur de lis represent these children who are always our link to the future. Let the chevron stand for the roof and protection of the House and lineage. Finally, let the rampant lion—dare we name him Aslan—signal the "Good News" which one generation roars or sings to the next. In this case, this book is one bit of the good news about human life as it was meant to be. (Editor's Note: See back flap of book jacket for the Joy coat of arms.)

# Contents

# Introduction

Last night Pastor Arthur Brown announced to the Official Board that Tom Kilburn has been recruited to serve as "Director of Youth Ministries" on our volunteer staff. "You may know that Tom's wife is a member of our church. Tom comes from a different background, but he has agreed to enroll in my next premarital counseling class." The board members laughed! Pastor Brown blushed, and wished he could recall the blooper. But I did not laugh. I don't think it was even a Freudian slip. "Joining the church" is a basic bonding matter—not unlike "marriage." And the membership class ought to have much in common with a premarriage class.

The basic thesis of this book is that *God's relationship with humans is one of intimate bonding, and that all human intimacies are "rehearsals" for the ultimate reunion of humans with their Creator.* Stated inversely, we might say that *all humans are bonding beings, such that their yearning for intimacy is an internal magnet which draws them, often unwittingly, toward God, for whose intimate relationship they are created.* You yourself have seen some of the most irreligious people you have known who are made mellow and tender in the ecstatic moments of life: at the birth of a child, or a grandchild; when they experience sexual loving; and in daily experiences when they find themselves being respected, treated gently, or touched.

The "case stories" told in this book are adapted from

real events and pseudonyms appear instead of actual names. No story is the unique story of any person or family. While every event is unique in one sense, I have not told anyone's story if it were the only case I had ever seen with that problem or focus. Human experience is very much alike, so the cases report common human situations. Some names used in the book are "real." All anecdotes about my own family, children, and grandchildren are reported straightforwardly. To test any name, check the Index. If the name is there, the anecdote or reference is unprotected reporting.

There is a sense in which this book has been written by the people across North America where I have been speaking, teaching, or doing seminars and workshops. I take people seriously and their questions and their hints become my agenda. Some of the best questions have come from anguished young people who huddled backstage with me after a lecture, usually beginning with something like this: "I think you could help me. Will you try?"

Then, some fifteen hundred of you responded when Dr. James Dobson first aired a presentation on "birth bonding" in which I addressed a Wesleyan congregation at Armbrust, Pennsylvania. Across the next two years, Dr. Dobson interviewed me face to face in a half-dozen sessions. And we talked almost exclusively about the issues of *Bonding: Relationships in the Image of God.*

Finally, I promised more than 2,000 high school people at the Stauffer Towers in St. Louis several years ago that I would write this book. They trusted me. I could tell by the breathless silence that overtook them in that great festival auditorium as I spoke.

I have winced when speakers and teachers have seemed preoccupied with the negative, taking critical analytical stances against almost everything. When anyone approaches the profound mystery of intimate human relationships with a focus on "encounter" or "conflict," I suspect they are feeding problems. "We had a good marriage," said a couple with whom we shared a Marriage Enrichment weekend, "but we wanted a better one, so we made a list of things to 'work on.' And immediately our marriage started going downhill." They were contrasting their own critical approach to improvement with the Marriage Enrichment program with its almost exclusive preoccupation with building on strengths already present in the marriage.

So, here I focus on "the good things." I talk about the basic relationships God has established, and about the intimacy and the bonds that flourish when we pursue the relationships as God intended that we do. But I also focus on "the good things" because there is vastly more good than evil in the universe. God called the whole creation "good" in the sense that it was complete and served the purposes for which each part was brought into existence. There is nothing "original" about sin and evil. Evil simply takes the good and distorts and corrupts it. I cannot name one evil deed which can be described in original terms, only in terms which describe how some good is perverted or destroyed. The "original sin" consisted of corrupting the good and of perverting the good "desire" into a fascination with evil. And the final "blasphemy against the Spirit of God" consists, ironically, of calling evil "good" and good "evil." That is why in this book I am not "on the attack." I do not play the part of the critic. And I do not want to focus your mind on "what is wrong."

There is a risk, however, in pointing to the good as the ideal. You may experience pain as you read *Bonding: Relationships in the Image of God.* Since all of us are dogged by imperfection, we may look at the vision of what is possible and experience it as "what might have been." We may be tempted to go away and cry, or to close the book and label the author naïve or insensitive. You may cry out, "But what about me? I was a premature baby and nobody touched me for two weeks!" Or, "What about those of us who didn't make it to marriage with our virginity intact!" Or, "Don't talk to me about 'one flesh' and marriage—nobody loves me at all!" Let me weep with you on the pages that stab you with memories of pain and failure. Much of what I write comes through tears. And the most ardent evangelists of the good, among those who respond to me, are those who have had close encounters with evil. One lovely young woman at a secular university said to me after I presented the pair bonding material, "I always hoped

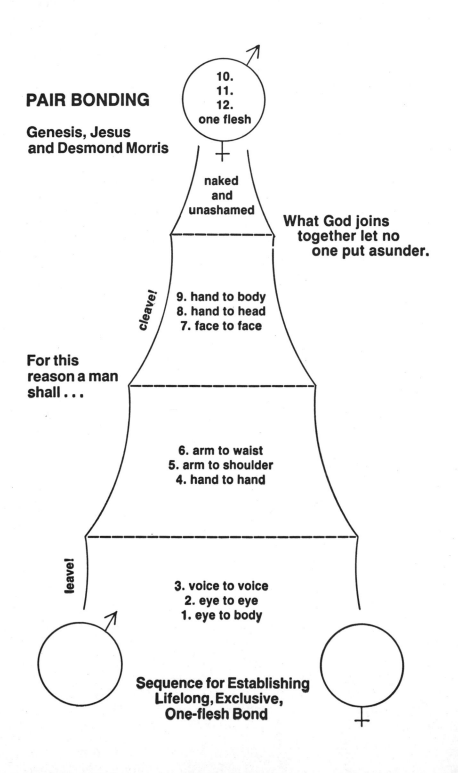

something like that was true, but I've grown up in the church, and no one ever told us what you have just documented in Scripture. If anyone had gotten to me, I wouldn't have had an abortion when I was sixteen."

When I face the question, "Shall I hold up the vision of ideal relationships in the image of God, knowing that all of us fall short?" I always come back to the answer, "Yes! Because we are inspired by the visions of perfection, even though they lie somewhere just beyond our absolute grasp."

At the end of each chapter you will find a section, "Questions People Ask." These will tend to pick up your questions, even your objections. I have gathered them from feedback sessions at college campuses, youth conferences, and parent seminars in local churches. And even now I am working on a manuscript which will focus on reconstructing broken bonds and dealing with the impact of a pornographic culture on the visions of intimacy and fidelity which are intrinsic to being human. If *Bonding: Relationships in the Image of God* is a book targeted on the impossible dream, then *Of Human Bonding: Coming Back When Things Go Wrong* comes back to earth and the way things are. But even reality is still under the summons to accept redemption and the call to follow the vision back to peace and innocence.

DONALD M. JOY, PH. D.
*Professor of Human Development*
*Asbury Theological Seminary*
*Wilmore, Kentucky 40390*

# BONDING

# 1

# *Who Is Holding Your Trampoline?*

△

"Here is an amazing test of 'personality health,' " I said
to my class of seminarians. And I described Dr. E. M. Pattison's "psychosocial kinship system" from the chapter on
"Health and Growth in Living Systems" in his book, *Pastor
and Parish.* I had drawn a picture of his idea as a four-
sided hand-held trampoline supported by four different
groups of people whom Pattison said we all have, or need
to have, in our system.[1] Bob stopped me after class:
"That's frightening," he said.
"What do you mean?"
"I can't come up with more than a dozen people in my
system, and one side of my trampoline has nobody holding
it at all!"

## We Need One Another

Look at that "hand-held trampoline." It says what everything else in the social world says—humans sicken and tend
to die if they are out of significant contact with other people.
That is true for newborn infants, but it is also true for all
of us at all ages. Dr. Pattison makes it easy to do a personal
check on our significant relationships. Before I outline the

3

system, take an even simpler test: If you were being admitted to the emergency room of your hospital, unconscious, with a life-threatening injury, who would need to be notified? Name and count the people.

Now look at the hand-held trampoline. Imagine it as a square, with five to eight people on each side. These sides represent four groups:

1. Family: first degree people such as parents, children, spouse.
2. Relatives: uncles, aunts, grandparents, and cousins.
3. Friends: your lifelong collection; but only those active today in your life experience.
4. Associates: acquaintances from work, from church, clubs, and recreation.

All of these must now be screened by five criteria on which significant relationships tend to rate quite high:

• There is a high investment in the relationship, with frequent face-to-face contact, and/or by mail or telephone.

• Strong emotional tone characterizes the relationships; you are not indifferent to each other. You would cross the street or spontaneously stop what you are doing to make time for friendly chatter.

• The emotional tone is consistently positive and affirming for both you and the other person. Pattison notes that a few "negative" relationships must be maintained, such as an unkind boss or spouse. The same might be said of parent or child. Otherwise, our support network needs and selects only positive relationships.

• The relationship has an "instrumental base." That is, both you and the other person know that in time of emergency the relationship could "cost something" and that you would make the sacrifice to help.

• The relationship is reciprocal and symmetrical. Healthy friendships are so evenly paired that both persons can give and both persons can receive and can do so without "keeping score." You find yourself saying, "Let's not talk about it. If this had happened to me, you would have done the same thing." This is a typical way of avoiding legalistic "re-payment" anxiety in a reciprocal and symmetrical associa-tion.

Now, what bothered Bob was that his trampoline had only about a dozen people all together, and one whole side was missing! Pattison has noted that the typical healthy per-son has about twenty to thirty people holding the trampo-line, and that there are an average of five or six people on each of the four sides. An exciting by-product of the healthy system is that about 60 percent of the people know each other. Who do you think introduced them, and under what circumstances?

In Bob's case, his "second degree" relatives were virtually all dead. But what we found was that he had, quite uncon-sciously, replaced them by developing close "surrogate" re-lationships that resembled those of "grandparent," "uncle," "aunt," and cousin.

Many of us are surprised to find that a healthy network of relationships consists of as few as twenty to thirty people. Although we tend to think that we must gather large num-bers of people around ourselves, in larger circles we actually tend to be more vulnerable. We might even starve to death emotionally from the lack of intimate support in a wide grouping of relatives and friends. In your own experience you have probably sometimes wondered where you could "bare your soul" when you were experiencing a private kind of grief or hurt. I am amazed that some people can blurt out very personal hurts in a larger group, but most of us need to look around the circle huddled in the narthex or in the parking lot to check the eyes of our listeners. We are checking to see whether we can trust our private grief or pain with these people. I call that caution "the swine test." Jesus, knowing that pearls are formed by painful and uninvited intrusions, warned us not "to cast our pearls before swine." If we open our hearts, we should know that the risk is that the pigs may charge into us viciously, wound-ing us further and trampling our pearls. I caution my "spiri-tual formation groups" not to make personal disclosures to the group until they experience a sense of absolute trust and discretion in the room. Don't risk the swine test with your valuable pearls.

A healthy system is dynamic in the sense that it is alive and always renewing itself. When a relationship is lost through death or by moving away, the network that is healthy undergoes change and replaces the lost intimacy over a transition period. The need for a healthy circle of friends drives us to reach out. We take inventory of our time and energy resources, reorder priorities, and take steps to give ourselves to new "others."

Systems that lack the four-sided balance or that are otherwise "impoverished," as Pattison would call it, tend to fall into one of two other personality categories:

1. *The neurotic system:* Here there are only ten to twelve people; some have died or live far away. Only about 30 percent know each other—the person keeps them apart and uses them without sharing them. The network looks like an incomplete wheel: the person is the hub, the spokes form a network, but there is no rim to connect the system.

2. *The psychotic system:* Here there are only four or five people, all focused on the "basket case" who demands almost constant attention. All of these people tend to know each other, since the central person requires constant supervision and care, and they arrange to leave someone in charge when they have to be out of touch for any length of time.

There may be two checkpoints for us. First, how many people do we have in our systems? The number is important, since we tend to lose our perspective on reality when the number declines. But a second checkpoint is equally important, namely: are the relationships reciprocal, liberating, and free from a sense of exclusive possessiveness on either side?

Most of us are frightened by such terms as "neurotic" and "psychotic." But, like all other words, they are only generalities, metaphors we have invented to describe real things that happen to people. So we might ask, "What kinds of things happen to people and what kinds of unusual behavior do we see in them that cause us to apply words such as *neurotic* and *psychotic?*" If we looked at roots instead of at effects we might not be so frightened by the labels. We might, instead, say, "This troubled person needs more significant people to surround him [or her], and enough people to provide the needed healthy perspective on life." Or we might try to understand how someone slipped into an unhealthy state. Who has recently been lost through death or job change or by moving? We might ask, "How could some of us surround the person with significant relationships? What intimate network could we wrap around the person?" A self-examination probe is appropriate, too: "With my present priorities, am I moving into a dangerous position of relative isolation? Am I investing enough time and energy in people on all four sides of my hand-held trampoline to maintain my bona fide membership in the human race? Has my recent loss, [job transfer, double load, or whatever] cut into the relationships base so deeply that I am in danger of trying to survive with an impoverished network?"

## We Need Quality Relationships

It is not surprising, of course, to note that at the heart of the gospel "joy" and "fellowship" have top priority. The Acts 2 story is one of instantly absorbing new believers into networks of communion, shared meals, and worship. And nowhere is the doctrine of fellowship articulated more clearly than in the first chapter of 1 John.

The internal structure of 1 John 1, like so much of Scripture, reflects an Eastern or "global" way of describing reality.[2] Westerners reading such globally structured material often lose their way, since generally we move from "parts to whole" in our ways of reasoning. In a global structure, the author first cites the big picture or the goal. Then, in reverse order from Western logic, discloses, step by step, the necessary sequence of adjustments which stand between the goal and a particular point where we might find ourselves on the spiritual pilgrimage. I have inserted the positive steps in the upward trajectory, so that you can see how the warnings are specifically targeted as negative alternatives if we make bad choices and forfeit the goal of fellowship and joy. So, Westerners are often helped by reading 1 John 1 backwards—verses 10, 9, 8, and so on. Note that translators who have not cracked the global picture either have to distort the obvious language the author used or to cover themselves in footnotes. Look first at the positive stair steps:

Verses 3–4: **Fellowship and Joy**
JESUS' GOAL FOR US!
We proclaim to you what we have seen and heard, so that you also may have fellowship with us. And our fellowship is with the Father and with his Son, Jesus Christ. We write this to make our joy complete.

*Read up.*

Verse 7: **Walk in "Light"**
CLEANSES FROM SIN AND GIVES
FELLOWSHIP
. . . if we walk in the light, as he is in the light, we have fellowship with one another, and the blood of Jesus, his Son, purifies us from all sin.

Verse 9: **Confesses Sins**
FORGIVES US AND ESTABLISHES
PERSONAL RIGHTEOUSNESS
If we confess our sins, he is faithful and just and will forgive us our sins and purify us from all unrighteousness.

To grasp the difference between the Eastern and Western perspective, imagine that you are looking at a photograph of a snowcapped mountain. You are planning to travel on a path that will take you over its highest peak. When I backpack on the Appalachian Trail or Kentucky's Sheltowee Trace, I much prefer to study the profile maps which show the relative elevations of every step of the trail I am looking at for a day's journey. But I also carry topographical maps with their curious markings which disclose elevation through cracking the code by carefully examining the two-dimensional markings.

If I am studying a two-dimensional map of a great mountain such as Pike's Peak, I may miss the actual "structure" of the mountain. I may even mistake it for a deep and treacherous hole in the terrain. But if I correctly identify the highest point on my flat map, I can then work my trip planning to my advantage. Eastern thought "sees through" what looks to Westerners like a flat topographical map. In 1 John 1, the snowcapped peak is "joy and fellowship with God who is Light!" And we will have to read down the mountainside in a descending, sliding manner to get to the bottom. But if we had a profile map, our eyes would spontaneously (as Westerners) begin with the perspective of ground level or verse 10—where we all begin on the ascent. It should not surprise us that Western exegetes do not with any consistency crack the code of the Eastern, global, top-to-bottom kind of analogy. However, this passage, along with the instructions for building the portable tabernacle (moving from the central "holy of holies" outward to the perimeter wall of the camp) should serve to alert us to trying the Eastern perspective on Bible passages which show any sort of potential sequence or progression.

We sometimes imagine that God's interest in us is primarily doctrinal or moral: that God wants correct belief and correct behavior. This is especially true if we imagine God to be a severe monarch residing somewhere above the celestial Supreme Court in a dictatorial or Big Brother sort of posture of surveillance and execution. What is clear here in 1 John and throughout all of Holy Scripture is that God's primary concern is to engage us in the healthiest of all possible relationships. Both "sins" which damage relationships through destructive behaviors, and "sin," which contaminates inner motives, are booby traps which prevent quality relationships from flourishing.

So the words *sins* and *sin,* like the psychological terms to describe troubled people, are metaphors we need to stand on their heads to discover what they really mean. It is clear here that "sins" are those behaviors and practices which tend to damage or to destroy intimate and honesty-based relationships. And "sin" denotes an inner set of attitudes which contaminate relationships—like a hidden bag of darkness carried around on the inside—which needs to be cleansed. Instead of thinking of them as theological constructs we might simply ask:

1. What are those behaviors which prevent quality relationships from being established and from growing? (Focus on *sins* as destructive behaviors.)

2. What are those inner motivations, those self-centered attitudes which contaminate relationships, conspire to control, and eventually go on display as behaviors? (Focus on *sin* as an inner motor rooted in the deformed self, sometimes called "the original sin" from which we need to be "cleansed"—in contrast to *sins* from which we need to be forgiven and reconciled to the persons impacted by the destructive behavior.)

So here in 1 John the stair steps are clear:

• Telling the truth about our destructive behaviors—*sins*—brings forgiveness and immediate purity and God's gift of personal righteousness as a first prerequisite to healthy relationships with both humans and with God.

• Walking in continuing transparent honesty brings us to the inner sanctification of motives—"purifies us from all sin"—to reduce further the booby trap to relationships.

• We are comfortable with the Light—"God is light; in him there is no darkness at all"—and we are suddenly into the vestibule of the most splendid of all communities: "Fellowship with us [the apostle and the faith community]. And our fellowship is with the Father and with his Son, Jesus Christ. We write this to make our [or your] joy complete."

"Fellowship with us" as a major goal of Christian faith may seem a bit unspiritual. But, from the Creation, we are created for significant and intimate relationships. God's first question following the tragedy of Genesis 3 was "Where are you?" God's experience of the Fall is thus marked by grief over the loss of a companionship that had been characterized by daily conversation and open honesty. There is no "vertical space" indicated in the Creation picture of the God-human relationship: God is Parent and Friend, but not dictator or monarch in any remote, vertical sense.

Look again at 1 John 1 to check the warnings which are scattered along the way:

(1:3–4: FELLOWSHIP AND JOY!)

1:6: **Deception**
CLAIMING FELLOWSHIP, BUT
LYING!
If we claim to have fellowship with
him yet walk in the darkness, we
lie and do not live by the truth.
(1:7: CLEANSING)
1:8: **Dishonesty**
REFUSING RESPONSIBILITY FOR
INNER "SIN"!
If we claim to be without sin, we
deceive ourselves and the truth is
not in us.
(1:9: FORGIVENESS)
1:10: **Denial**
INSENSITIVE TO GOOD AND EVIL:
OUT OF TOUCH WITH WORD!
If we claim we have not sinned,
we make [God] out to be a liar and
his word has no place in our lives.

In this chapter I have wanted you to look at your own
relationships. I wanted you to treasure your personal, hand-
held trampoline—that network of people who keep you in
touch with the real world. And I wanted you to see how
Jesus calls you to honesty in all relationships, and how what
we sometimes call "salvation" or "grace" is really a grand
scheme by which all of life can be focused on the one goal
of the Creation: that humans may live fully and intimately
with other persons and with God.

## QUESTIONS PEOPLE ASK

*Q: Does the trampoline principle apply lifelong? Can
children develop such a network?*
A: I suspect that infants look much like Pattison's description of the psychotic. They are literally basket cases, and
a small group of people dedicated to their survival make
certain that at least one person is on the job at all times.
In a similar way, the adolescent years tend to be impoverished because other people are hanging on to only two or

three sides of the trampoline. Teenagers have simply not lived long enough to fill up a minimum vanguard of lifelong friends. Notice how fanatically they hang on to their age-mates, yet typically they will not even know where a half-dozen of those people are ten years from now. We have often structured our schools and churches to isolate our teens and our children in sterile friendship environments. All of us need age-mates, but we are impoverished if we have contact only with people who are locked in to the same vocation, the same schedule, and the same set of daily stimulations as our own. Yet that is what we do with our children for the first eighteen years of their lives. A small nuclear household, or a single parent home, each with a typical "one and a half" children, is an impoverished environment, too, separated as most of them are from significant relatives. The network idea is useful for checking the healthfulness of our systems, but it is also helpful in making informed decisions about where to live, what kind of extracurricular activities to encourage, and what sort of church and community agencies into which we wish to invest time and energy.

*Q: I'm surprised that you suggest twenty to thirty people as the "normal" network. I thought we were supposed to be closely tied to large numbers of people, and to treat them all the same.*

A: I was surprised, too, to read Dr. Pattison's observations. But I was also relieved—liberated, perhaps, is the better word. Many of us work with large numbers of people. I have to learn an average of more than fifty names each month, just to know the people who register in my courses, not to mention another five hundred each year whom I see every day but for whom I have no teaching obligation. Yet, when graduation day rolls around, I can always sense that I have a very special attachment to a small handful of students—five or six—that simply does not exist for all of them. I suspect that I am not alone; but it is a pleasure now to own the trampoline and to say to myself, "These are the people on my 'work place, clubs, and so on' side of the trampoline with whom I have rejoiced, wept, and laughed. They will always belong to me in some special way, and I to them, but I do not possess them." So each June, I always go through a mild sort of postpartum separation trough, and prepare to pick up a new set of work-place friends in the next season. I worry about some professions which have traditional taboos against establishing any significant relationship with colleagues or clients. It should not be surprising to us if these isolated people develop some strange behaviors if their trampoline is abandoned along one side. But, no, I'm afraid we cannot invest the energy to sustain a much larger network than twenty to thirty persons. However, we can be significantly "for others" in our vocations, lifestyles, and in the practice of Christian care and ministry.

*Q: We just moved from the West Coast, and I think my trampoline has been devastated. Is the sadness I am feeling related to this whole thing Dr. Pattison is talking about?*

**A:** I am sure that your "homesickness" for California is one signal that your trampoline has all but collapsed on one side—your immediate "work-play-worship" network. So, just when you feel least like it, you need to establish new and significant relationships. Many people become less socially active in a new community and impoverish their well-being, even their health.

*Q: My mother is recently widowed. She phones or I phone her at least once a week, but most of the time she begins with a rehearsal of all of the funerals she has attended in the last few days. I worry about her "state of mind," but she is otherwise pretty healthy. Is her "trampoline" the problem?*

**A:** All of us face the "death" of our trampoline, I suppose. But when grief of a severe personal nature strikes the number one side of the support system, followed closely by losses in other sides—relatives, lifelong friends, and work-play-worship associates, the effects can be devastating. The "neurotic" system and the "psychotic" system then loom as frightening trends for the elderly.

# 2

# *On Splitting the Adam!*

△

Sam walked from the emergency room to the parking lot of the great hospital. Sue was dead. Ten tons of automotive steel in a tangled head-on crash were too much for her. Sam checked his watch: two in the morning. A siren wailed in the distance. *Another tragedy,* he thought. Somewhere not far away tree frogs sent heavy vibrations through the night air. Exhausted, without language to blurt out his anger and his frustration, he leaned against a car and studied the night sky. She was gone. Occasional well-formed clouds were making their way across the sky against a full moon. Gone. *For ten years we have lived and moved as one person; now Sue is gone. In all the universe I will never find her. I could search behind every cloud, walk every square foot of the surface of this planet or the moon. Sue is gone. Gone. And she will never come to me again. Life as I have known it has ended. . . .*

Any human being, left alone, will eventually ask whether life is worth living alone, whether one can retain sanity alone. "Solitary confinement" is among the most severe penalties. Prisoners of war who survive with their personality intact often describe detailed fantasies and reconstructions they used to keep up at least an artificial contact with signifi-

14

cant persons in their networks or trampolines as we called them in chapter 1. In this chapter I want to look as far back as possible for the roots of this social need of humans. It is appropriate that anthropologists and sociologists look backward into the fossil age to document records for such things. I want to take the quantum leap back theologically, to examine who Adam was and why Adam was created with the characteristics we read about in the first three chapters of Genesis.

My plot line for this chapter is fairly simple. It runs like this: God wanted to create humans for personal relationships. This meant that a "symphonic" relationship would have to be rooted in similar personhood. The creation of humans is described in Genesis 1 as being "in the image of God." In Genesis 2 the human receives "the breath of life." So the second plank of my plot line is this: The personhood of God is "full spectrum." The human personhood would also have to be "full spectrum," or at least created in a way that would make communication and intimacy possible and desirable both for God and for humans. Finally, the plot line expands in this chapter on the discovery that Adam, created in the image of God, and blown to the shape of full humanity by the "breath of God," is—in a crowning act of creation—split: The female is differentiated and taken out of Adam, leaving the first male as the residual remains of what I will call "Alpha Adam." Later in the chapter I will introduce the "Omega Adam" Christ, whom the apostle Paul referred to as the "second Adam." I will show how, in a similar way, the "Bride" is differentiated out of "Omega Adam" and the theological foundations of both human sexual identity and of the nature of Creation-Redemption history may take on a bold and significant new dimension.

### The Good News: The Alpha Adam

These are days when most of us are a bit uneasy about opening the topic of sex differences. And, traditionally, the Genesis creation material has sounded quite sexist. A male God creates a male Adam, and history is off to a male-chauvinist beginning.

Long ago I was poking around the authorities looking

at the meaning of "image of God."[1] I was writing a book, *The Holy Spirit and You*, at the time, and I wanted to get it right. I had been trained at one of the best seminaries, so I knew the biblical and theological meanings: to be re-created in the image of God is to be renewed in righteous-ness, in holiness, and in knowledge, after the image of the One who created us. Eventually, I stuck by those definitions, but I had to turn my back on one theologian's simple obser-vation: that in the context of Genesis 1, it is clear that what-ever else the image of God may denote, it is intrinsically rooted in our being created "male and female." I recall that I chuckled, closed the book, and referred to my memo-rized text about the image of God. Such simple interpreta-tion, I thought, was on the same level of another author who had quipped that if we had only Genesis 1 for context, we would know that creativity is the human gift of the divine character. So I went theological in my writing.

I am older now, and I have come back again to reexamine the image-of-God/male-and-female concept. But I had to learn the reality of it the hard way. I had to come back to it inductively by trying to unscramble what has gone wrong with families. Children, it turns out, who lack the effective impact of both sides of the image are almost always deformed in their abilities to respond to God. I now con-clude that the first Adam was both male and female, and that the Genesis 2 record is a way of telling how the female was differentiated out of the male. I hypothesize further that by separating out the female from the male, both were magnetically charged to draw them back to the original unity or wholeness. You can see that if this is related to the "image of God," as Karl Barth insisted that it is, both male and female witnesses are essential if we are to get a full spectrum representation of what God is about.

As I said earlier, our understandings of God must be cut loose from notions of dictatorial, monarchial, and vertical distancing between God and humans. Although most bibli-cal images of God are not vertical, such political notions have contaminated Christian thought from the political sec-ular environments which influenced major theologians. The God of Creation is principally described as doing parentlike things: making/creating, rejoicing in the quality of the creation, walking with the humans in the cool of the day, and calling out "Where are you?" This Creation picture of God is one of a caring, dialogic, intimate person who enters into human experience, rejoices with them, and eventually grieves at the breaking down of the intimacy.

The original Adam, what I am calling here "Alpha Adam," was a single human being, yet seems to have contained the elements for the paired creation. Nothing could be more obvious than the message in the surgical metaphor of Genesis 2: from a solitary and lonely person, by means of the surgical opening of the "side," the female is differentiated and removed, leaving the still-anesthetized male to awaken and discover his "other self." All of this double-Adam message is underscored by the New International Version's rendering of Genesis 5: "This is the written account of Adam's line" (v. 1). It goes on to say in verse 2 that when God created humanity, God made the human in the likeness of God, and "created them male and female; at the time they were created, [God] blessed them and called them 'man.' " But the footnote tells the truth—"man" is really "Adam." The word is used before the differentiation and is always inclusive of male and female, but the male "Ish" calls the female "Issha" at first sight, and Ish cleaves to Issha (not "wife"). Only after the Fall does Adam become the term for the male alone, and he "names" the woman "Eve," thus announcing his control over her as they have "named" the rest of Creation earlier. It may be important for us to get the language straight here if we are to deal with "sexism."

The original Creation dream was of a man and a woman who were joint tenants or co-regents. Both were blessed. Both were charged with "having dominion" in the creative management of this planet. Every bride and groom are constituted "prince and princess," even if it is only for a day. Yet the dream lives. If we do not understand the double witness—male and female—written into our humanity, we will distort our understandings of God and imagine that God is male. God, like the Alpha Adam, either is neither male nor female, or God is both. But we are so culturally trapped in our generic gender words that we may miss this first lesson for humans in the doctrine of Creation.

Sometimes we think that God could not have made a mistake and created a single human in the Creation, where everything else was "male and female." But, of course, everything else was *not* male and female. Biologists report that there are hundreds of thousands of living species which reproduce without gender and without fertilization. There are species of fish which literally change sexes in the absence of a male, since the same body can be differentiated to provide the male source of fertilization.[2] It is strikingly egocentric of us if we imagine that God *had* to make humans male and female, since there was no possible way we could have been created otherwise! And Genesis 1 and 2 may be telling us, among other things, that humans were split into two genders for more profound reasons than for sexual reproduction.

Suppose that the real reason for creating humans both male and female—for the splitting of the Alpha Adam—had to do with distributing the splendid full-spectrum image into parallel and complementary packages. Suppose further that some aspects of God's character are best illustrated by a female, and that some are best illustrated by a male. All this adds up to a magnificently rich portrait of God. And, as always, the metaphor written in the male and female humans is likely only a pale representation of the reality toward which they point.

Now we can imagine that the male side of God's image and the female side of that image are sufficiently different—intrinsically different—that they may be magnetically charged and attracted to each other. This magnetic pull may be fueled as (1) the search for balance and completeness as each "half" yearns for its matching counterpart; or (2) the sense that coming together makes a cosmic statement or nonverbal witness to the character of God, who created them partial facets of a grand image which is larger than either of them.

What this suggests further is that there may be a core of intrinsic differences between male and female, and that those differences are elegant statements about the complex and glorious nature of God. We may now have come to a profound moment of truth. But we are not alone in our search for those intrinsic differences in gifts and graces.

The common folklore answers it in either of two ways, and both are extremes: (1) Men and women are different and that means they are locked in to specific roles, functions, and values; or (2) the differences are pure mythology; they are only descriptions of culturally imposed expectations and demands. I find neither of these folklore solutions very helpful. In a later chapter devoted to fetal development, I will describe what seem to be nonnegotiable, physiologically rooted differences between females and males. Although those differences undergird much of what are popularly thought of as sex differences, they are not identical to the popular mythological view.

What we do know about adult sex differences allows us to affirm two things:

• We are always impoverished when a single sex group meets, discusses, and makes decisions, since only part of the full-spectrum personhood seems to be present. The suggestion that women should be full partners in discussing and setting policy for the control of nuclear weapons is one piece of popular wisdom which gestures toward this need for mutual dependence of males and females.

• The healthier the adult is, the more experience the person has acquired, the more nearly that person approximates full-spectrum personhood. One Benedictine Abbey close to me subjects its young priests to rigorous examination in a full acknowledgment that a young male at, say, twenty-five years must be pretty healthy in every way to deal with sexual energy and the celibacy vow. And the amazing Harvard-based study which gave us the famous *The Seasons of a Man's Life* reports that four polarities undergo a new construction in the mid-life transition which brackets on either side of age forty.[3] This mid-life mellowing must harmonize the tensions between:

1. The "young" versus the "old."
2. "Destruction" versus "creativity."
3. "Masculine" versus "feminine."
4. "Attachment" versus "separateness."

The men who mellowed out were those who were able to embrace the threatening pole at the end of each set.

So, by mid-life, as grandfathers, it was typical that these men were more affectionate with their grandchildren than they had been with their children. The Benedictines remind us that the Christian vocation perhaps calls all of us to life-long healthy personality and demands that we somehow manage to embrace: (1) aging and the aged; (2) contemplation and use of imagination; (3) the opposite-sex set of sex-rooted behaviors and attitudes and values; and (4) a life-style which liberates others and which practices lifelong philanthropy—sets them free—by differentiating the self from others, from vocation, and from activism.

The Creation is put together, however, in such a way that sexual differentiation occurs from the moment of conception and pretty well organizes life agendas until about mid-life. This means that most of us will be cradled in the arms of nicely polarized fathers and mothers. We may ask, then, what God has distributed to females and what is given to males to carry out their human vocation as "image of God" representatives.

Females, it appears, tend to organize life around "affect" and "affection."[4] There is a tendency for women to make moral decisions around people issues—who will be hurt, how close is the person to me, and how could I change the outcome to spare the most and especially the most important-to-me people from being hurt? I was shocked to find Jami Maree, my two-year-old granddaughter, empathizing with me when I accidentally severed a small artery. I was doing some remodeling, missed the wall stud with a blow of my hammer, striking my shinbone. Blood began pumping in a four-inch jet-thrust from the front of my leg. Only Jami and I were at home. I said, "I think I better go take care of this bad leg," and moved toward the house and the bathroom. Jami followed, watching from the doorway. This typically egocentric little woman, who normally needed a lot of my supervision, had turned her full attention to me. "Papaw be all right?" she asked, as I hoisted a foot into the lavatory to begin the cold water treatment. Her affective connection was attached to me here. We will see in the discussion of fetal development that the organization of the female brain may provide the root for this affection-based way of living. It may be significant (though how should we discover it) that the Genesis 3 tragedy is a chronicle of the seduction of a woman by a verbal manipulation of her "reason" while subjecting her to a person-to-person assault on her affections or feelings.

Males, on the other hand, have long been observed to organize much of life around issues of justice and objectivity. It would be easy to assume that a woman's umbilical attachment to the young would orient her to affection-based life decisions, and that the relatively detached way the male is related to conception, birth, and child care would tend to shape him into a more concrete, thinking type. But the studies do not suggest that these differences are absent at any age.[5] From the moment of birth, as we will see later, the intrinsic differences related to attachment and detachment seem to be present. The male Adam was susceptible to Eve and seemed helplessly drawn into the "original sin." But it may be significant that the seduction was dialogic and affection-based—introducing the attachment to a new "god" in wisdom and in the new relationship with the most gloriously beautiful being present in the Creation. Although the male Adam may have been more objectively grounded and less susceptible to the relational seduction, he was vulnerable to the one significant attachment in all Creation: his magnetic spouse.

## The Tragic News: The Original Sin

If the male and female were created as joint tenants and co-regents, the bliss was temporary. Eden would become a memory and a dream. The memory would haunt all of us with the thought that life could have been better than it is, that relationships could have been based on respect instead of under the threat of power. The dream would haunt us because we see the hope in the eyes of our young. We see their innocent imagination that a life of love will be perfect and constant. And we know that Eden is doomed to fail them, too. They, like us, will fall into an adversary relationship, and joint tenancy and co-regency will evaporate. The Genesis picture traces the tragic story. At first the Creation blessing and charge was to both the man and the woman:

> God blessed them and said to them, "Be fruitful and increase in number; fill the earth and subdue it. Rule over the fish of the sea and the birds of the air and over every living creature that moves on the ground."
> Then God said, "I give you every seed-bearing plant on the face of the whole earth and every tree that has fruit with seed in it. . . ." And it was so.
>
> Genesis 1:28–29

But, while the blessing and the charge were addressed to the man and to the woman together, the seduction by the serpent was uniquely the failure of the woman. The seduction of the man by the woman was a second form of original failure. The woman was seduced in her affections while listening to a rational line. And the man was drawn by his own attachment to the woman; the one distinctly affective dimension of the man's experience became his point of failure. Thus the failure formed a solidarity for the human species. Now examine the gender-specific aspects of the "curse"—the consequence of their failure:

> So the Lord God said to the serpent,
> "Because you have done this,
> Cursed are you above all the livestock
> and all the wild animals!
> You will crawl on your belly
> and you will eat dust
> all the days of your life.
> And I will put enmity
> between you and the woman,
> and between your offspring and hers;
> he will crush your head,
> and you will strike his heel."
>
> Genesis 3:14–15

Harold Myra has embellished the Creation account in his fictional piece, *The Choice.*[6] In it Myra gives us a picture of the serpent as a magnificent butterfly with multiple sets of multicolored wings attached to a highly colored fuselage. The fact that serpents as we now know them resemble such a wingless, footless fuselage makes the imagery very compelling. So also does the folklore from the zoology lab, which suggests that the bone structure of the snake may have once supported an undercarriage of feet.

At any rate, the serpent is doomed to a demeaning position in the lifechain on earth and is placed at an adversary position to the woman. It is not hard to see the root of the promise of a coming Savior who will crush the head of the evil one by his life, death, and resurrection. Nor is it difficult to trace the adversary relationship of evil to that of Jesus—when we daily witness the mindless destruction as the serpent strikes the heel of humanity as it draws the blood of seduction, addiction, injustice, injury, and death.

> To the woman he said,
> "I will greatly increase your pains in childbearing;
>   with pain you will give birth to children.
> Your desire will be for your husband,
>   and he will rule over you."
>
> Genesis 3:16

The consequences to the woman are the briefest of the three. They focus on issues of attachment and affection and intimacy. Oddly enough, childbirth is allegedly complicated by human moral failure. It is as if the cranium of the species was literally enlarged by the demands created by the human choice of learning by experience. This sense of "knowing" is intrinsic to the serpent's seducing lines, and constituted "becoming like the gods." We know that it is the delivery of the baby's head that makes human delivery so hazardous to the mother, a condition that does not exist in such an extreme form for any other species. And we know that it is uniquely human to possess a brain with the capacity to do reflective, formal, three-dimensional thinking, all of which are essential for thinking that is truly moral.

"Your desire will be for your husband" hardly sounds like a curse.[7] Most men wish their wives had hearts only for them. While some interpretations reach for a more complex solution to the mystery of this consequence, it yields to one powerful insight if you simply ask, "Where was her desire/affection supposed to be rooted?" It is clear that the woman's vulnerability to attaching to the wrong persons/objects led to her fall. Yet she is created female specifically because such a fully charged image of loving attachment is essential to represent the character of God. Therefore, her penalty will be that she will be supremely attached to her husband. Watch the women you know who are blindly loyal to their husbands. One young college woman told me that she was inappropriately intimate with her man, but that she felt it was her duty to comply with his wishes. She had heard that doctrine at church, she said. But as much as a man might enjoy the total adoration of a woman, what he needs is not her idolatry, but her companionship. He needs her supreme attachment to be fixed on God. If it is, she can be a partner and a wife to him, and together—with supreme anchoring in God—they will be faithful to each other in affection and confrontation as well.

"And he will rule over you." Much popular teaching in the church moves on the assumption that male dominance is God's "plan for the family." But it is clear that male dominance is part of the curse. No doubt, young lovers are baffled when the first signs of male control show themselves, since in their dream state of *eros,* they imagined themselves in that idyllic world of co-regency and joint tenancy. Although a woman is likely to be motivated out of self-interest to assert herself and show her independence, it is almost exclusively a male tendency to try to control everything in sight. Look at the curse on the male, and you may begin to see why:

> To Adam he said,
> "Because you listened to your wife
>   and ate from the tree about which
>   I commanded you, 'You must not eat of it,'
> Cursed is the ground because of you;
>   through painful toil you will eat of it
>   all the days of your life.

It will produce thorns and thistles for you,
and you will eat the plants of the field.
By the sweat of your brow
you will eat your food
until you return to the ground,
since from it you were taken;
for dust you are
and to dust you will return."

Genesis 3:17–19

Here there is no reference to broken human or divine relationships. The man, it turns out, will simply be subjected to the harassment of the environment from which he will be destined to carve out his existence. That frustration will tax his Creation gift of objectivity to its limit. This male side of the image-of-God representation—which tends to excel at objective detachment, judgment/justice, and decision making without paralyzing emotional attachment—will tend, now, to be turned into an efficient machine. He will trouble-shoot the universe and will be driven with the urge to fix it, to make it run correctly. And here the tragedy creeps in. Woman, God's special differentiated gift, presented to the male at the moment of his postsurgical awakening, now is confused in his frustrated mind and blurs into the category of "property." His capacity for being a workaholic, spending his days and nights fixing the external world, tends to turn on her to fix her! The ultimate way to control her is to put her out of the house, to do violence to her, or, equally as painful to her, to replace her with another woman. The new woman, perhaps, so the dream goes, will be more cooperative, will share the dream of managing Eden.

So the consequences to the woman seem to focus on the internal and the affective. For the man they are relatively external and objective. In each case their moral failure at the Fall occurred at the point of attack to their most limited gifts. Now their penalties are custom made to match their primary differentiated gifts. They are left distinctly polarized as female and male, but those distinctive gifts are warped: the female to inappropriate submissiveness, and the male to inappropriate dominance.

Now none of this is to suggest that men and women are totally different from each other. And it is the wildest heresy to canonize the Fall and proclaim it as "God's plan for marriages, for family, or for the human race"! But we can make appropriate responses both to the Creation design and to the distortion brought on by the original sin.

Look, first, at the way things *are*, in relation to the way they were designed to be: God's design was for joint tenancy and equal/mutual value. And "Ezer" as the "helper" suitable for the man is an elegant word describing one who comes down to walk alongside the man to deliver him. It is used most often to describe how God helps the humans, and it is conceptually linked to the idea of Paraclete or "divine counselor," which Jesus used to describe how the Holy Spirit will work. But the fact is that virtually every man-woman relationship, beginning as it does with this innocent sense of mutual respect and joint tenancy, tends quickly to shift toward a vertical, hierarchical deformity. The woman tends to be inappropriately attached and dependent, even to worship and adore the man, and she tends to lose her direct and clear attachment to God. And, in the face of frustration, the man tends to regard the woman as simply another part of the material world over which he must sweat, labor, and exert control—he succumbs to a mere functional view of woman. She tends to try to manipulate the relationship by the use of the subjective, the affectional, and even by alien attachment. He tends to try to manipulate the relationship by the use of power, just as his brawn and sweat are the hallmarks of the fallen man. It is a simple step for the man to add to his collection of material goods an additional woman (or more) on the sheer hope that he can find one piece of female "property" that will not frustrate him. Thus, the woman's characteristic is to display deformed and manipulative affection, while the man's characteristic is to behave as if a woman is mere property to be controlled and owned.

Jesus was quick to point out to a group of men who regarded women as property that they had forgotten the doctrine of Creation. Here we face the fundamental importance of the image-of-God teaching from Genesis: We are called to be renewed in the image of the Creator. This calls for new kinds of relationships between men and women. It calls for women to be repaired, in affect. Her desire must be for God's own image in her life, for the daily presence and intimacy of the Garden communication with God, and for that affection to control all potential alien attractions. It calls for men to be healed of their curse-bound tendency to regard all persons as objects and their wives as their chattel slaves. To be redeemed is to be under reconstruction in one's view of the self and of others. Joint tenancy and co-regency are the summons both of the original Creation and of the New Creation.

## The Best News: The Omega Adam

It would be easy to miss, but there must be a significance in the fact that God made two Adams. Paul sees the first Adam as the door by which sin entered the world; the second Adam, Jesus Christ, is the door by which we are delivered from sin: "For just as through the disobedience of the one . . . the many were made sinners, so also through the obedience of . . . one . . . the many will be made righteous" (Rom. 5:19). But Paul also makes the point that what God has done in giving us Jesus is "better than" what we would have possessed in the original Adam, even if that Adam had never sinned. Anglo-Catholic theologians even speak of Adam's "happy Fall." It was happy for us, not for Adam, because it evoked God's abundant grace, which, in a morally sensitive world, brings in God's Son and the intimate life with God which is now opened to all people.

There is no question that Jesus of Nazareth was born a baby boy. He grew to manhood, learned a man's trade, behaved in every way as a secure male—there is no "macho" behavior in the record, but he lived out the image of God characteristics of a Creation-shaped male. In his parables and one-liners, it was common for Jesus to refer to himself as the "groom" on his way to the wedding, even late for the wedding. He saw his teaching years as similar to the bachelor party that precedes the wedding. We have no hesitation in thinking of a male Jesus: baby in a manger, boy in the Temple, carpenter in Nazareth, master designer of winds, and calmer of seas. But we get images, even specific metaphors, to suggest the other end of the Adam spectrum. Jesus "breathes" on the apostles as if charging them as Spirit-filled agents of God's re-creating work. The imagery is exactly analogical to the Genesis 2 inbreathing of Alpha Adam. And Jesus sits looking down on Jerusalem, brooding on the lost energy and the mission coming to an end: "O Jerusalem, Jerusalem, you who kill the prophets and stone those sent to you, how often I have longed to gather your children together, as a hen gathers her chicks under her wings, but you were not willing" (Matt. 23:37). The metaphor is distinctly and intrinsically feminine; it is classic "encompassing" gesturing.

In earth's darkest hour, the Omega Adam hung dying on a cross outside of Jerusalem. At last the soldiers came. With a single incision, Jesus' side was opened, just as Alpha Adam's side had been. From the first Adam, woman was formed. From the Omega Adam, the Bride appeared. Suddenly, Roman art, exposing the "heart" of the wounded Jesus, becomes profoundly metaphoric: the subjectively attaching "Mother," the "Bride," the "Church" is the "other half" of Jesus. And it is that Bride half of Jesus which is present and active in the world today. It is in the Bride that we are conceived, born, nurtured, and umbilically attached to Mother Church. These are real and inward attachments, but there are appropriate liturgies in which, by ritual and embraces, Mother encompasses us as if to say to us in a thousand ways, "You belong to us, and we will never let you go."

It is this Bride and Mother that Jesus separates out of the Omega Adam and leaves behind, following his resurrection. At the ascension, the risen Jesus explicitly instructs the assembled believers to wait until the Holy Spirit comes upon them. That event will mark the actual differentiation of the Bride from the Groom, reminding us of Eden. The Bride will then serve as the continuing, uninterrupted witness to God's incarnation and salvation in Christ.

With the full-spectrumed personhood of Jesus as Omega Adam established, it becomes clear that Jesus is both Groom and Bride, and that Jesus' presentation of God's image to us is uniquely full-spectrumed. God did it twice—once in Eden, and finally in Bethlehem: both Alpha and Omega!

In this chapter I have wanted you to embrace all of Scripture and one of its major themes and metaphors. God has written the primary witness to the full-spectrum personhood of God into the human species by clustering and differentiating major gifts into the two sexes. Having given us the "first curriculum" of our first parents to represent God to us, God then extended the metaphor and reminded us throughout history that he is married to Israel—that oftenwayward bride who plays the harlot with heathen nations and pagan ways. Yet, like Hosea who was married to a woman who practiced prostitution, God was persistently seeking his bride to woo her back.

History began in the Garden, with the union of a woman and a man in the primeval wedding, under the spell of the image-of-God magnet that draws the male and female together for a wholistic witness to God's nature. And history will end on the banks of a river, at the Marriage Supper when Christ the Bride is received and joined to Christ the Groom, when Body and Head are reunited—and in the placenta all of us will be present who are being re-created in the full-spectrum image of God.

## QUESTIONS PEOPLE ASK

*Q: I would like to accept the idea of co-regency and joint tenancy, and I can see it both in Creation and in Jesus as both Groom and Bride. But isn't it true that Paul teaches that the husband is the "head" of woman? How can both ideas be reconciled?*

A: You are on to an important principle, that all Scripture must be reconciled with itself. Don't let anyone move you from that as a sort of first principle. Much of religious confusion arises from selective proof-texting. And some go so far as to say that what is at the end of the Bible supercedes anything that goes before it. Those people will insist that their misunderstanding of the apostle Paul sets aside direct teachings of Jesus. Remember, too, that the big picture is more important than more isolated apparent contradictions. And some apparent contradictions may be understood in the context of the written material or of the circumstances the words were addressing. The apparent conflict with the idea of "headship" is almost entirely a matter of misunderstanding what the term means in Paul's times.[8] Our first clue comes in looking at the confusion that Paul projects if we take our own meanings to his words. Look at a passage in Corinthians, for example:

> Now I want you to realize that the head of every man is Christ, and the head of the woman is man, and the head of Christ is God.
> Every man who prays or prophesies with his head covered dishonors his head. . . . For this reason, and because of the angels, the woman ought to have a sign of authority on her head.
> In the Lord, however, woman is not independent of man, nor is man independent of woman. For as woman came from man, so also is man born of woman. But everything comes from God.
>
> 1 Corinthians 11:3, 4, 10–12

I have condensed the extensive discussion about "hair" and the covering of the head. It is clear that prostitution and hairstyles had created a serious problem of miscommunication through appearance—not entirely unlike our confusion in the 1960s when certain hairstyles became associated in the public mind with drug use. It was required in Judaism, for example, that men wear a linen head covering, but a recent convert who still wore his hair in the style of male prostitutes in the village would distort the clear message about his changed life. I point out this context for the passage to help us focus on the critical issue for us and our doctrines of Creation-Redemption and of Groom and Bride.

Paul's idea of "headship" is obviously not the same as that of General Motors' idea of "president." Our first clue is in the fact that the opening triad is not in hierarchical order. If it had been a vertical listing, it would have read:

The head of Christ is God.
The head of man is Christ.
The head of woman is man.

It could even have continued the chain of command which is so popular today: The head of children is the woman. But by giving the order so as to sandwich the humans between the divine shows an idea different from vertical sovereignty. The word *kephale* which gets translated "head" has a primary meaning of "source of life or strength, or 'origin.'" So, in Colossians 1:18, Christ "is the head of the body, the church." In Colossians 2:19, Christ is the source of life who nourishes the church. In Ephesians 4:15, we are to "grow up into him who is the head, that is Christ." And here, in 1 Corinthians 11:3–16, the discussion focuses not on a vertical or power relationship, but on derivation. Hence:

> The source for man is Christ.
> The source for woman is man.
> The source for Christ is God.

This search for "roots" established, Paul goes on to weave an argument against long hair on men:

> A man ought not to cover his head, since he is the image and glory of God; but the woman is the glory of man. For man did not come from woman, but woman from man; neither was man created for woman, but woman for man. For this reason, and because of the angels, the woman ought to have a sign of authority on her head.
>
> 1 Corinthians 11:7–10

In an amazing argument which a sexist reading would find most perplexing, Paul is arguing that the woman's hair is her "crown," and constitutes a special "authority." To a chain of command reader, the best cracking of the text runs in a circle. Then, using the "however" of a closing summary argument, Paul sets the record straight; neither man nor woman is independent of each other. While Eve is formed from Adam, so Adam is born of Eve. And everything comes from (is derived from) God (vv. 11–12).

*Q: All of this stress on parents as the first curriculum makes it pretty hard for widows, widowers, and other single parents. Where do they fit?*

A: The fatherless and the widows are always the special concern of God. This is true in the Old Testament and it continues in the New. I will want to talk more directly to the issue in chapter seven–"Parents and Children: For Each Other." But a short answer is this: The church is the "family of God," and every single parent and every fatherless or motherless child should be able to say with Psalm 27:10, "Though my father and mother forsake me, the Lord will receive me." The faith community is populated with back-up fathers and mothers who can stabilize both children and solitary parents. If this is your next urgent question, look ahead to chapter seven.

# 3

# Pair Bonding: What God Joins Together

△

"I've got to talk to you." The college freshman who was operating the video camera and recording my session had lingered after everyone had left the campus auditorium. "When you described 'father-absent daughters,' I saw through a problem that is driving me crazy," he said. We synchronized our calendars for the three-day period I would be lecturing in his city. Then, talking in his borrowed car while consuming Big Macs during his lunch hour, David explained: "See, Ellen's parents went through this messy divorce when we were finishing our sophomore year—fifteen years old. They even sold the house and both moved to opposite ends of the country. My mom asked me if I thought it would be all right to invite Ellen to live with us to finish out the year at school. Of course, I thought that was a great idea. Well, we were both Christians, but with both of my parents working, within a month we began having intercourse at home after school. We repented every time and promised that we would never do it again. But we always did. And even though we knew it was wrong, Dr. Joy, it was awfully good."

"Do you know why it was good?" I asked. "It was because

you were made for that. But the timing was terrible, and you were taking enormous risks with yourselves."

"I know," he went on, "but she lived with us until we graduated from high school two years later. Then, when she went to live with her mother fifteen hundred miles away, I thought I would die. So I packed up and took the bus. I got a job and a room, but I couldn't make enough on minimum wage to keep afloat. I phoned my best friend from high school, and he came to join me to help pay the rent. I got him a job on a different shift where I worked. One day I came home and found him in bed with Ellen. I could have killed them both right there. But instead I threw his things into his suitcases and put them in the hallway and told him to get out. He left. Then Ellen and I got accepted here at this college. We knew we would live in the dormitories and have really good supervision, so we would have to stop having intercourse. But, after a week here, Ellen said we should date around. I didn't want to date anybody else, because I was so attached to Ellen. But I agreed. And Dr. Joy, did you see her tonight? She was on the front row, right in front of you, hanging on to the guy all the time you were talking. I know what is going to happen. This is the second guy she's dated, and it is driving me crazy, because I know they are going to be in bed together."

"You're on to something, David," I agreed. "She is a troubled woman. Many daughters of divorce are very fragile and very vulnerable to sexual intimacy because they are so desperate to have a man—any man—to make them feel loved. You were the one who was there when Ellen was shattered by her parents' divorce. And the 'absolute privacy' led, as it usually does, to 'absolute intimacy.' But God's glue was very powerful for you. You are a pretty healthy person with standard-equipment kinds of affection. You have been well loved and are capable of giving love. Let me play off a scenario for you. You are the person who introduced Ellen to sexual intimacy and pleasure. You are profoundly attached to her. That means that you probably have the resources and the motivation to 'heal' her. I doubt that any other man could do it so well. And if she isn't healed in a good man's arms, she is likely to become a promiscuous woman and a very unhappy one, too."

David's anguish became so deep that he transferred at the end of the semester to a college near his home. And Ellen, upon returning for her second semester and finding him gone, left school and moved in, again, with David's family.

In this chapter I wish to talk about the "glue" by which God mysteriously "bonds" a man and a woman. From Creation it is clear that there is a developmental pattern in the bonding: leaving, cleaving, one flesh, naked and unashamed. To this I wish to add the twelve-step sequence observed by secular zoologist Desmond Morris and reported in *Intimate Behaviour*. Morris, regrettably, sees no Creation mystery and he answers to no moral or spiritual summons, but his observations about how humans establish intimacy that can last a lifetime are helpful to us. Morris is also a self-styled anthropologist, often highly speculative. More "specialized" scientists tend to criticize Morris, but they tend to offer no observations at all about the intangibles which hint of Creation mystery.

The primary source I offer here is, of course, the Judeo-Christian foundation for what some secular observers have recently named "pair bonding." It is first observed in the Genesis 2 picture of Adam magnetically rejoined after sexual differentiation. Then, Jesus, in Matthew 19:4–6, quotes Genesis, adding, "What therefore God has joined together, let no man put asunder" (v. 6 RSV).[2]

## Bible Versus Science?

You may wonder whether it is right to look at the work of scientists—anthropologists, biologists, and zoologists—in trying to understand what God is doing in the mystery of Creation and especially in the sensitive matters of human intimacy and marriage. So, if you ask a question about using "science," it is a good one. Let me tell you how I work.

I hold to the idea that God has left three witnesses in our world:

## REVELATION WITNESSES

1. *Creation:* the whole universe around us.
2. *Scripture:* the inspired writings of the witnesses, given and kept by the Holy Spirit.
3. *Incarnation:* the words and works of Jesus of Nazareth, God's Son.

If all of these come from God, we may be sure that all of them agree. Science is the strategy that humans have devised for unravelling the mysteries of the Creation. Theology is the strategy that people have developed for making sense out of the witness which has been given to us in Holy Scripture. Christology or soteriology is the science to which we have devoted ourselves in order to get inside the meanings of the birth, life, words, actions, death, and resurrection of Jesus of Nazareth, God's only Son.

Most of the time all three of the witnesses agree: Creation, Scripture, and Incarnation. When we look at human pair bonding, for example, they all seem to agree. But sometimes the witnesses seem not to agree. Look at the conflicts now raging between those who call themselves "creationists" and "scientists." But we may be sure that the disagreement is a direct result of (a) looking at only part of the total data; or (b) imagining that any one of the witnesses by itself tells us everything we need to know about God's witness in our world. Anyone who wishes to look at the big picture must keep all three witnesses in focus, since God made them all. If I discover what seems to be a disagreement in the witnesses, I may be sure that the apparent problem is either a problem of my own perception, or that I am working with blinding presuppositions, bad theories that keep me from seeing what God revealed clearly in Creation, Scripture, or Incarnation. Or I may simply be dull and stupid.

I must, therefore, work with a hermeneutic of "suspicion"

directed at my own work: my science, my theories about Creation, my perceptions from Scripture, and my understanding of the Incarnation in Jesus. It may be that I have not yet been able to ask clear and well-informed questions, or that I am misreading the data in front of my eyes. I am surrounded by a good deal of bad psychology, poor anthropology, and geology. Science is no better than the questions that scientists are able to ask, and questions are always limited by the imagination and curiosity and the world view of the people who are asking the questions. But, just so, I am also surrounded by a lot of bad theology, too, because one's theology is no better than the quality of imagination and curiosity and the world view of the theologians. If they are as microscopically preoccupied with Scripture as the scientists often are with the Creation, neither the theologians nor the scientists may be able to help us with the really big questions. We all have to do our own work and listen to all of the witnesses. We can know for certain that when all of the facts are in and the witnesses have yielded up their last messages, they will all agree. We can affirm with Paul's letter to the Colossians, that by Jesus, the Son of God "all things were created: things in heaven and on earth, visible and invisible, whether thrones or powers or rulers or authorities; all things were created by him and for him. He is before all things, and in him all things hold together" (Col. 1:16–17).

## Is Pair Bonding Marriage?

We sometimes say of a couple such as David and Ellen that since they have been sexually intimate, they are the same as "married." I find with some young people who are caught in the bonding pattern that their ideas about intercourse and marriage are not at all clearly differentiated. "We were engaged," one young man told me, "so we just said the words like they are in the marriage ceremony, and we both agreed that we were really married after that."

It is my judgment that neither Genesis nor Jesus is talking about legal marriage. Legal marriage and legal divorce are both temporal matters which are regulated by prevailing customs and laws. Marriage is a necessary legal arrangement if a society is to maintain social order. But the Creation magnet works, and "what God joins together" is a magic formula that applies to any intimate relationship, whether or not the relationship has been regulated by the social order. Those of us who are sensitive to protecting the ultimate values, then, are obligated to look at the profound, universal issues behind marriage and behind divorce. Jesus insists that we are responsible to protect the bonds which God has formed by the Creation. It would be a terrible thing for parents or well-meaning friends to be guilty of "putting asunder" what God had glued together by Creation design and charter.

I have been honored to perform dozens of marriage ceremonies in my career as a minister. Until about ten years ago, I was always filled with a surge of power and authority when, at the end of the liturgy, I laid aside my Bible and ritual and grasped the right hands of bride and groom in my own two hands. Then, gazing full into the faces of the witnessing congregation, I would intone: "Forasmuch, then, as John and Mary have consented together in holy wedlock, and have declared the same before God and this company by the joining of hands and the presentation of rings, I therefore, by the authority vested in me by Almighty God and recognized by the Commonwealth of Kentucky, do hereby pronounce that they are husband and wife together in the name of the Father, and of the Son, and of the Holy Spirit. What, therefore, God has joined together let no human put asunder!" Then, to the groom, "John, you may salute your wife." And there before the community they permitted us a glimpse into a microcosm of their intimacy—they embraced and kissed. The intimacy symbolized the public promise that they were taking full responsibility for each other, that property, children, and all legal matters now had a proper foundation. And, with the community of faith, they were also promising to acknowledge God as the Author of love and grace and to walk with us as participants in the larger family of God.

Today, when I perform a wedding, I still say all of the

same words, but I know now that the authority belongs to God: "What, therefore, God joins together let no human put asunder!" refers not to what *I* have done, but to the Creation-based bond that may now be consummated. I serve only as the oracle to pronounce God's extravagant work in the couple's relationship. I also serve as the deputy for the legal and civil state, which has a stake in what happens in human intimacies, since items of name, inheritance, insurance, hospitalization, social security, a host of details, not to mention descent of children and property are important matters for its courts. But I serve primarily as the "minister of the Gospel of Jesus Christ" and call the community to witness the amazing Creation grace which continues to attract and to bond a woman to a man and the husband to the wife. There we celebrate that grace and also invoke the redeeming grace of God to continue to protect and enrich the lives of these two, now become one as they join us in the journey through an alien environment toward that splendid City of God and the final Marriage Supper of the Lamb.

## Protecting the Bond

It may be helpful to picture the pair bond as the jewel and the marriage as the ring or other setting which has been designed and formed to display and protect the jewel properly. Or, on a vastly different plane, think of the pair bond as an expensive automobile, and the marriage as the garage in which you protect it. You can park the car on the street, of course, but the risks to such a choice are enormous—vandalism, theft, and the inevitable corrosion that unprotected weathering brings. These are serious threats to your auto. If you value the car at all, you will want to protect it. Ideally, you will see to it that the contractor has completed the garage no later than the day your fine new car arrives.

We have a little difficulty translating Judeo-Christian social regulations into current North American or Western European settings. In Jesus' time, the betrothal/engagement constituted a legal and binding contract, but sexual intimacy was absolutely forbidden until a second ceremony and wedding rite was observed. During the betrothal, the woman could terminate the agreement for any reason. But the man could not change his mind without going through a divorce procedure. All of this is played out for us at the end of Matthew 1, when the conception of Jesus is reported. The pregnancy produced a complication for Mary—a scandal—and for Joseph, whose problem was that he was now betrothed to a woman who was not a virgin. A bride's virginity was the responsibility of her father, right down to the proofs of that innocence. You can read about it in Deuteronomy 22, for example.

It is curious, too, that the Old Testament gives us no word at all about what happened if betrothed couples became intimate before the marriage was made final, or if experimenting young people became sexually active. The silence may suggest that (a) careful community control over conditions in which the young and the betrothed might have access to each other (not unlike the days in North America, not long ago, when a chaperone simply accompanied lovers to defuse inappropriate intimacy); or (b) social custom by which the young were spared extended contact by matchmaking (in which the families contracted well ahead of the years when surging sexual desire might be set afire by courting or by having to search out a suitable partner for oneself); or (c) community common sense, by which inappropriate intimacy was immediately covered by legal marriage. In any case, the community values ruled out sexual experimentation or sexual promiscuity. It is clear that Old Testament penalities for sexual predators were severe—normally the death penalty for both persons involved, thus extinguishing the possibility of promiscuity triggered by inappropriate intimacy experience. In the one case at the end of Deuteronomy 22 where the death penalty was not required, the illegal, forced intercourse was immediately protected by public marriage. The man was forced to make a silver payment to the woman's father, and he was notified that he could never divorce her for any reason. The final notice was no doubt rooted in the fact that unprotected intimacy often triggers lifelong appetites for illicit sexual experience, and since the male had seduced her, he was barred from recourse to claiming any rights to divorce her for sexual promiscuity. In our contemporary cultural settings, we may be sure that we will want to look at the relationships between pair bonding and legal marriage and to chart a pattern of action, perhaps even starting up new traditions, which both affirm and bring into reality the practices which encourage chastity, fidelity, and lifelong family solidarity for ourselves and for the generations to come.

There is a sense in which parents feel responsible for delivering virgins to the marriage altar. We symbolize that pure condition by dressing brides in white, but we might improve our delivery system by more carefully reading the signals of their ripening affections. Every human being has dreamed of virginal love—of one man and one woman who had no other partner. With this unbelievably high aspiration among our young, we might do them and ourselves a favor by unfolding the blueprint of developing intimacy. Desmond Morris, with his twelve steps of pair bonding, may help us keep faith with the young by showing the predictable path a relationship will take. Zoologist/anthropologist that he is, he may also help those of us who are gatekeepers at the community of faith to learn the signals which cry out for public sanction and endorsement, saying, "Get us to the church on time!"

## Pair Bonding in Perspective

In Desmond Morris' book, *Intimate Behaviour,* he reports that the twelve steps in pair bonding tend to be present in all human cultures. He notes that variations from the twelve steps tend to move people toward more violent sexual behavior. Morris also cautions that when steps are missed in the rush to genital intimacy, the bond tends to be deformed and to break. We will all recognize, in looking at the steps, that the first journey up the staircase tends to take the longest time. In that first sequence we tend to find ecstasy at each new marker. If a person leaves one relationship and goes quickly to another, the steps tend to be accelerated, with some even skipped. And a person who has reached genital intimacy in one relationship tends to move even a naive partner quickly to genital intimacy almost immediately in any future relationships.

We will find our vision of marriage enhanced by the studies in bonding in another way. Many people regard marriage as a matter of such seriousness that a couple should approach it much as they would a business contract. Thus "partners" or "spouses" should come together to ensure a financially stable and well-ordered relationship. They should be sufficiently mature, old enough, and with enough social experience to make a good husband or wife. However, even a casual look at the anthropologists' word on pair bonding suggests that the glue of God's Creation defies logical, businesslike analysis. When the mystery bond of Creation is present, two people are enabled to survive all kinds of adversity. Let Desmond Morris say it:

> To say that "marriage is a partnership," as is so often done, is to insult it, and to completely misunderstand the true nature of the bond of love. . . . In a partnership one merely exchanges favours; the partner does not give for the sake of giving. But between a pair of adult human lovers there develops a relationship like that between mother and child. A total trust develops and, with it, a total bodily intimacy. There is no "give and take" in true loving, only giving. The fact that it is "two-way giving" obscures this, but the "two-way receiving" that inevitably results from it is not a condition of the giving, as it is simply a pleasing adjunct to it.[3]

What is even more troublesome for us is that the anthropologists faithfully report that our high premium on so-called social experience is contributing to patterns of promiscuity and its defective bonding. Our divorce statistics are likely more related to the amount of unprotected pair bonding—and to social pressures to be sexually active before marriage—than to any other one cause. The parental and faith community side of the issue may find us stressing secular standards (age, economic assets) above the personal and affective values. In some cases parents insist on breaking up, using contraceptives, and even having an abortion, instead of protecting an otherwise treasured bond with marriage. Pair bonding may show us that we have sacrificed the one mystery which would have sustained the young lovers for a lifetime. "What God joins together" has very often been "put asunder" for relatively trivial, and secular reasons.

### "LEAVING"—No Physical Contact:
### Steps One, Two, and Three

There are twelve steps in Desmond Morris' observed scheme. They correspond, overall, to the sequence laid down in the Judeo-Christian blueprint. In Genesis 2, which is quoted both by Jesus and Paul, there are three distinct movements:

1. *Leave* father and mother/Morris, steps 1–3.
2. *Cleave:* cling/hug spouse/Morris, steps 4–9.
3. *Union,* one flesh, naked, unashamed/Morris 10–12.

The first three of Morris' steps are specifically "no touch" in character. You have often seen them occur relatively quickly, perhaps in an hour or so. These early steps are clear indications that the person is "leaving father and mother," who serve as our primary source of bonding or attachment. Here, in innocent attraction, we can watch the progression move. Typically, these steps move quickly. The remaining nine steps require greater time investment if the bond is to progress in a healthy pattern and last a life-time.

*1. Eye to body.* This is not a "sexual look." It is the "Eureka!" look of discovery. It cries, "Where have *you* been all of my life?" The magic of this discovery moment is that the taste is unique. Rarely do two people discover the same "other." It is typical, too, that the first moment is preserved lifelong in a memory photo—a stop-action photograph engraved in the mind. When I do premarriage counseling, I always begin with a call for each to share that snapshot. They are amazing, and the rehearsal of the memory sets the couple on solid ground. The memory photo is often a close-up and only partial, much as Piaget's phenomenon of "centering" characterizes childhood perception. We often say, "Love is blind" or "What does she see in him?" It is precisely here that the love bond defies logic. Love sees some aspect of the person or the personality; love sees what the person might become with the help of a lover who truly believed; and love sees, as my Grandma used to say, "more than skin deep."

Bonding affection likely is so grounded in God's grace that it is given eyes to see the possibilities within the beloved person. "Wait until we are married. Will your parents be surprised at what is going to happen to you!" is a threatening gesture toward the family, but it is also the cry of an artist who sees possibilities that perhaps no one else on earth can see. Surprisingly, very often those visions become reality, and many of us have become whole and gifted persons quite beyond the reach of imagination, and have done so in the hands of our lovers.

2. *Eye to eye.* If the angels are kind, lovers discover each other at the same time. If the mystery hits simultaneously, they will both know the quickening heartbeat and flush of slight embarrassment, and the relationship may begin at once. But if the discovery is one-sided, there may be long days or months of gazing without the return of the magic look. It happens both ways. But, in either case, it always comes as a bit of an embarrassment to be caught gazing at someone, only to find him or her suddenly turning to look directly into your own penetrating eyes. The feeling must be like that of peeking through a keyhole and finding an eye on the other side looking at you. Gazing into the eyes is rather an infringement on privacy, for the eyes are, in fact, the keyhole to personal secrets. Here, early in the discovery of a potential relationship, the eye contact is brief. At step seven, we will see that eye communication dominates over all other. Conversely, relationships or marriages that are falling apart become obvious because the couple is never found looking directly into each other's faces when they talk.

3. *Voice to voice.* How do you say "Hello" to someone you have never met? Ask lovers how they met. "I went back to that stupid restaurant three times because I wanted to catch the attention of a certain brunette waitress, but she clearly thought I was a clumsy clod." More typically, among the young, there is a phone call or a frantic plea

to a friend in the powder room: "Please! Will you find out whether he has even noticed me?" The cultures which many persons value most develop formal strategies for people to meet without embarrassment. Today, the "matchmaker" is less a marriage huckster than a social agent in many cultures. My sons during junior high and senior high days enjoyed the safety of trusted friends—usually their church friends of the opposite sex—who would do the "checking out" for them. By whatever method, it is the voice-to-voice stage that comes next, and usually it comes quickly.

At thirteen I hailed my barber at a Nazarene revival meeting where I was visiting. He gladly gave me the girl's name and her father's name. I could do the rest with the local telephone directory.

Today's affluent family often installs a second private line listed as "teenager's phone" to accommodate to the importance of voice-to-voice. In one of his classic sequences, Chip of "Hi and Lois" fame is on the telephone. His mother objects that he has been talking for two hours. "Who is it?" "Mary Lou Treadwell." At his mother's insistence that he should go next door to talk to her, Chip objects: "Hey! I'm not ready for that!" Indeed. And it is important that relationships not be pushed at any point. The reluctance of either or both persons is clear indication that the basic formation of the bond is still "green" and more time is needed. Should anyone attempt to make sense of the content of all the voice-to-voice material that passes early in a relationship, it would all turn out to be trivial. Only much later will substantive conversation develop. For now, Chip's two hours on the phone after school will seem a waste of time. And the whole world agrees that when a young man has not found enough voice or language to speak one complete sentence to his parents in the last month, it is surprising how verbal he becomes with his own "Mary Lou." But then, the first Man was evoked to the first coherent speech at the sight of Woman. Perhaps such behavior is historically noted; it may be intrinsic to males.

While these first three steps in pair bonding seem simple, even naive, they may be useful to us as a check list for studying the deteriorating relationships we encounter. In

most cases, bonds that are falling apart lack the critical behaviors of face-to-face conversation in which eyes meet and
hold their gaze, and the magic of that first glimpse may
have entirely disappeared. This often leaves only the furtive
touch of love-making episodes, which, having little bonded
foundation, tend to leave both persons dissatisfied.

### "CLEAVING"—First Touch: Steps Four, Five, and Six

Kissing, Morris reminds us, tends to move a relationship
to a sexual focus. Hence, only conventional kissing should
be present, if at all, through the first six steps in the establishing of the pair bond. A conventional kiss is one used in
traditional "Good-bye" ceremonies on leaving or returning
home. This second set of three steps brings physical contact,
but none of it is directly sexual. Indeed, the couple will
tend not even to look directly into each other's eyes before
they move out of this set. If they add an embrace to "Good-
bye" or "Hello" ceremonies, it will be without the important
face-to-face grounding which comes later, and the embrace
is potentially troublesome as it may awaken specifically sexual feelings ahead of the appropriate schedule in the bonding process.

4. *Hand to hand.* While touching hands will later have
explicitly romantic content, it does not intrude itself here.
The couple take hands to make a social statement: "The
two of us are together." "Make way for us; one seat will
not do, we need two spaces at the concert." "Neither of
us is up for grabs; think of us as being together." All the
same, four square inches of human skin—the palms of their
hands—will, in fact, be touching. The bonding is now helped
along by galvanic skin-to-skin contact. The two may be
vaguely aware that the skin contact has quickened the imagination, and that being a couple feels much different from
the endless hours spent separated on distant ends of the
telephone connection.

5. *Arm to shoulder.* It is not yet a hug, but there is a
gesture of "ownership" in the arm across and around the
shoulder. It extends the social statement: "We have a special
relationship. We do not object to your inferring that the
friendship is going somewhere." Yet there is no face-to-

face or other intimate contact—only the upper shoulders have been added to the hands.

6. *Arm to waist.* While athletes may make the gestures of the huddle with arm to shoulder contact, they less often move to close the gap between the bodies in the arm-to-waist embrace. The couple at this point pull the bodies close. But we observe that the faces are still forward. They seem to be looking at us or at the outer world. In fact, they tend now to drop the head slightly, to talk as into a hidden vault positioned somewhere between them. They will be posing questions and giving answers that range from trivia to remarkably personal disclosures: "What are you going to do when you are through school?" "Do you like peanut butter pie?" "How many children do you want to have?" "Where do you want to live?" The questions and the responses are endless. And it is critical that the vault have an absolutely foolproof lock. If either partner repeats the quiet disclosures among other friends, the bonding is interrupted and may be fatally flawed.

Bill told me of his frustration: "I would like to ask Alice to marry me, but every time she goes back to the dormitory, her roommate pries everything out of her. I feel like we have to start over every time we see each other. It is as if we have been robbed."

I watched a couple at the entry door of our favorite pizza house. It is hard to imagine how they got through the door. He weighed over two hundred pounds and she was about average size, but they were almost literally glued at the side. If they had been fitted with a hip bolt four feet long that replaced all four sockets, they would have looked the same. I wondered how they would sit down. But as the young man swung her in a ninety-degree turn, her feet lifting off the floor, they approached a booth. There both squatted slightly and they retained the side bond right into their seating.

It is during this sixth step, arm to waist, that enough of the life visions of each are disclosed that a decision about the future of the relationship is urgent. This is the "last exit" on the pair-bonding freeway. Any "emergency exit" down the road will almost certainly leave skid marks of grief and pain through which both persons will need to work. With step six, a checklist to evaluate the relationship might be appropriate:

1. Does my partner's vision undergird and strengthen my values, my beliefs, and my lifestyle?
2. Does my life vision fit my partner's life vision?
3. Are we "good" for each other, motivating for good?
4. Am I comfortable with my partner's expectations about me—fulfilling my partner's vision?
5. Does my partner see me having a legitimate place, other than "being there" for my partner's use?

If any of the above evokes a negative response, it is very likely time to say, "You have been good for me. I want to thank you for being a good friend. But you deserve someone who can dream your dreams with you and can give a whole lifetime to helping you fulfill them. I am not that person."

### Still "Cleaving"—Intimate Contact: Steps Seven, Eight, and Nine

The Old Testament concept of "knowing" describes how Eve knew Adam, and how Sarah knew Abraham. There were other terms to describe sexual contact: Jacob "lay with" Leah, or Amnon "raped" Tamar. Sexual experience which is not grounded in extended and shared life experience through light touching and long conversation is not the ultimate intimacy. In the intimate steps of seven, eight, and nine, we see the couple now turn toward each other. Communication is vastly different, but there is no direct sexual contact. Direct genital contact during this time will almost certainly bring on intercourse and will foreclose completion of the bonding process for months or years to come. In addition, the unprotected intimacy tends to expose the relationship to high levels of anxiety. It also tends to introduce an undercurrent of mistrust which can haunt the marriage.

7. *Face to face.* Desmond Morris calls this step "mouth to mouth." He does so because intimate kissing occurs here. The kissing, Morris informs us, immunizes the digestive sys-

tems of the partners by exchanging the benign bacteria which each carries. But the kissing is also the first of the steps to introduce sexually arousing courting behavior. We are still several steps away from genital contact, so the restraint now is critical. I call this step "face to face" because there is much more than kissing on the agenda. If they had progressed to this step, my friends in the pizza parlor would have touched only lightly at the door, if at all. Entering the booth, they would have faced each other. They would have cleared the ash tray and the candle. Leaning forward, they would have gazed into each other's eyes. I asked Bette whether the personality profile seemed to describe her fairly accurately. She turned to look at her young friend Bob. I expected to hear them discuss whether the profile paragraphs were, in fact, on target. But after perhaps ten seconds of deep gazing into each other's eyes, they turned to me and, in unison, nodded their affirmation. I had the distinct feeling that if an X-ray camera could have captured the actual amount of communication that had passed in those few seconds, it might have run to the thousand pages of an encyclopedia. The long investment in the first six steps provides a basis both for "knowing" and for nonverbal communication. The couple is now less likely to spend endless hours in conversation, but to read each other's faces.

8. *Hand to head.* Who would have thought to count, as a separate step, the freedom by which lovers touch the face, stroke the hair, trace the edge of the ear, or cradle the head during kissing? Morris makes the point that the head is the most vulnerable part of the body, the most likely to be struck in a mortal attack. Hence, he thinks, humans have learned to take care into whose hands they trust their heads. Samson neglected to count the cost of trusting a woman he did not truly "know." Ask yourself who touches your own head. Your barber or hair dresser, perhaps, although you tend not to return to such a professional if you have your head handled unnecessarily. The Anglican priest blesses children at the communion rail by touching the head. The head is handled in all rituals of Christian baptism; and the bishop or other ordaining person invests authority by the "laying on of hands." When you have counted these,

there remain only parents, grandparents, and others who have passed the test for being trustworthy. So the lover is highly trusted when access to the head is given. I watched a dear friend of mine, dying of cancer at the age of eighty. His wife, the love of his youth, came through the door for her daily visit. I watched as she approached the bed for what I thought was a conventional kiss. But as she reached to kiss him on the cheek, I saw him begin to nibble her ear. I left the room. I knew I was in the presence of something too intimate to sustain the gaze of even a close friend.

9. *Hand to body.* Morris explains that this "knowledge of the body" excludes the genitals. There is a sense in which this step might better be called "respect for body" or even "knowledge of the body." At this final step before "naked and unashamed" freedom breaks over the pair. There is ultimate appreciation for the body configuration, the way the person occupies space—height, weight, pigmentation, hair follicle patterns, imperfections of complexion or physiology. It is the person who is known and respected, not some phantom of perfection.

When I became aware of her broken engagement, I tried to console Denise. I had first met her some three years before she arrived at college. Now she was to be a senior and her graduating fiance had broken their engagement with the explanation that he was not sure of God's will for him. He was taking a year of retreat to seek the will of God. I foolishly suggested to Denise that I had a young seminarian in mind for her to date. She wisely demurred, "I would like to meet Bart, but I don't think I'm ready to date anybody. See, I'm still very attached to Dallas, and I really hope he finds out God's will soon, because then he can think about us again. Besides," she went on, "Dallas is the only guy I have ever gone swimming with." Although I was baffled at this criterion, I did not respond. Then she went on, "I've seen Dallas dripping wet. I know he's got bird legs. And he has a mole on his left shoulder blade and a small toe that laps over the fourth toe. I would recognize those feet anywhere." I was speechless. Denise was aware of a deeper level of attachment than I had ever contemplated.

I told the Denise-and-Dallas story when Dr. James Dobson was interviewing me on "Focus on the Family," a radio talk show.[4] Dr. Dobson was moved to tears and interrupted me to tell of the night his father died. When the emergency room physician came to notify Jim's mother that her husband was gone, she asked, "May I spend some time with my husband?" The physician agreed to prepare the emergency room for her. Then, Dr. Dobson said, "My mother spent forty-five minutes with my father's body. She stroked his hands, traced the outline of his feet, his face, and kissed him. She was saying good-bye to the body she had known. It was not primarily sexual, it was total knowledge that had sealed their marriage across the years." Exactly. So I suggest to lively teens that they look closely at the next group of senior citizens they encounter at a rest stop or in a restaurant. "Imagine which of them is just what you will look like. Try to think why anybody would really love you after you lost your youthful body, became bald or gray, wrinkled. Some of you will suffer surgical deformity through amputation, radiation therapy, or worse. What will hold your love together then? The only glue to take you through the years will be God's Creation bond that never breaks."

With step nine, we come to the final point before which the bond needs absolute legal protection. With a relationship in motion, it becomes critical to "get them to the church on time," and to provide the resources of families and of the community of faith to guarantee safe passage into the ultimate intimacy.

### "ONE FLESH"—Naked and Unashamed: Steps Ten, Eleven, and Twelve

The final three steps belong only to the couple. They deserve absolute privacy to match the absolute intimacy which legal marriage guarantees to them. Even when there is no legal marriage, a developing bond will strongly tend to move ahead into the naked and unashamed phase of ultimate intimacy. Lovers often equate their lack of inhibition with each other with lack of guilt for having risked sanity, community stability, and both past and future gener-

ations by consummating a sexual relationship that is unprotected and therefore potentially destructive.

10. *Mouth to breast.* Desmond Morris, zoologist and anthropologist grounded in the evolutionary hypothesis, as-
sumes that humans have "risen" from other primates. He
is baffled that the extended and gentle touching between
an adult human male and the adult human female have
no links to breeding behavior in the monkeys. He describes
the approach behavior of male monkeys and notes that

> the only body contacts, apart from actual genital interaction,
> are the mechanical holding actions by the male's hands and
> feet. He grips the female's body, not as an amorous intimacy,
> but to steady himself while he makes the rapid pelvic thrusts.[5]

In stunning contrast, human intimacy universally includes
the use of mouth and hands to caress the partner. Morris
observes that among all species, it is only the adult male
who establishes an intimate relationship with an adult female. The male's approach to the female's breast may, indeed, be rooted in his memory of dependency upon
mother's breast and milk. But it may be a transition from
"cleaving to mother and father" to "cleaving to the spouse."
The gesture suggests dependency, in any case.

Remembering that the male readily takes responsibility
for the protection and defense of the female, especially
while she is bearing and caring for their young, it may be
a stroke of transparent honesty for him to reduce himself
to a position of weakness as he suckles the breast. It is as
if he were saying, "I will always draw my strength from
you. I depend on you. You don't know how weak and dependent I feel. But you make me strong." Such feelings are
at least acted out in the gesturing of even the most arrogant
and confident executive types. The Man may be saying to
the Woman as in the Eden Creation: "We were formed
separately, and I have always known that while I must protect you, it is really you who gives me the courage and
strength to be the Man."

Whatever the gesture may mean, it is clear that in the
Judeo-Christian vision, the sexes are mutually interdepen-

dent. In 1 Corinthians 11, where Paul is discussing "headship" in terms of dependency and identifying the sources of strength, he reiterates the Creation-established mutual dependency: "In the Lord, however, woman is not independent of man, nor is man independent of woman. For as woman came from man, so also man is born of woman. But everything comes from God" (vv. 11–12).

11. *Hand to genital.* With sexual arousal under way, the hands also spontaneously search out and caress the final private space: the genitals, with their pleasure resources. It is not uncommon for first contact to bring rapid sexual climax, especially to the male. Normally the exploration of the genitals is the threshold to intercourse. Unmarried partners who prize technical virginity sometimes stop the bonding sequence here if they have crossed the boundary between steps nine and ten.

12. *Genital to genital.* Penetration and sexual intercourse completes the pair-bonding sequence. The intimacy begun at the moment of birth with first skin contact between parent and child has been transposed to a key in which are repeated many of the same gestures, but now with an adult companion in a second and more glorious bonding. It is not surprising that sexual intercourse then sets up the possibilities for pregnancy and a new launching of the intimacy cycle that begins with birth and its parent-infant bonding.

## Epilogue

Two and a half years after my original conversation with David, I found myself in a guestroom on the edge of the great city where he had grown up. I checked the huge telephone directory and found his name. The phone call put David and Ellen in my room within thirty minutes. Beaming, now married for more than a year, Ellen was roundly pregnant. They told of grand fulfillment in their marriage, their work, and especially their joy at serving Jesus through the junior Sunday-school class they taught together. I learned that they were more than tithing, out of the sheer ecstasy of having their lives centered on Jesus.

At the first silent spot in the conversation, which focused mostly on David, since I had never personally met Ellen, I turned to her: "Tell me. Is David good to you?"

Ellen beamed. "I took my shower first last night. Then, while David showered, I just fell backward on the bed to pray. I had worked all day, and the pregnancy is getting uncomfortable. I found myself praising God. I was saying, over and over again, as I so often do, 'Thank you, Jesus, for giving me a man who will never let me go.'"

Although I was not exactly speechless, I was silenced. David had pursued the bond, and Ellen was now indeed a peaceful and gracious woman of God. "We can hardly wait to see where God is going to lead us," David kept saying as they were leaving me that night. "But we know it will be exciting and it will be good."

## Lifelong Bonding

The pair bond may appear to be a series of twelve steps through which a couple may move toward the target of ultimate intimacy in sexual intercourse. But the twelve steps are more than a delivery trajectory; they are a daily agenda for maintaining a treasured relationship. The intrusions of television, the rearing of children, the crowded social schedules and the demands of our jobs tend to chip away at the strength of our bonds. Healthy marriages require continuous traveling over the pair bonding sequence. Troubled partners may not have looked into each other's eyes in weeks or months. Deliberate looking, touching, and setting aside time "to be apart" for "ourselves" become important strategies if our relationships are to endure and increase in the quality of intimacy.

In this chapter I have wanted to distinguish between pair bonding and marriage, and to show how marriage is essential to provide an adequate protection for the jewel of pair bonding in a relationship. And I have wanted to marshall the witness of Creation, Jesus, and Desmond Morris to let them agree on the mystery and wonder of human marital bonds. In the next chapter I will draw on Melvin Konner's observations to discuss what has gone wrong with the bonding.

QUESTIONS PEOPLE ASK

*Q: Are you suggesting that any couple who comes to genital intimacy should get married?*
A: Not quite. Yet, the first question to ask when a couple has been to intimacy is, "Should this bond last for a lifetime?" It is easy to say no for a lot of reasons that have nothing to do with the good of the two people involved. If they have anything to do with age, economics, or social status, I would recommend that those issues be put in the deep freeze while the really substantive issues are examined. These include:

• Has a dependency developed in which each of the partners works better, is more imaginative, spontaneous, and generally healthier when the other is present—in the room, for example?

• Are they willing to take full responsibility for the emotional needs of the other partner?

• Are they ready to take deliberate steps to participate in their own economic support or that of the larger family which surrounds them?

We imagine in North America that marriage means leaving the nest and supporting the full weight of all responsibilities after that. This has never been the Judeo-Christian view of how the family works. Parents who withdraw family resources during the launching phase are buying into a pagan perspective of maturity, not a biblical one. They need to contemplate that the pagan culture provides contraceptives, abortions, and free access to premarital lovers, taking almost purely an economic view of marriage. Many Christian parents have bought unwittingly into the pagan economics without intending to push their young also into the pagan morals. We may not be able to have it both ways.

When I discuss the future with couples who have been all the way to genital intimacy, I ask these kinds of questions: (1) How do you think your relationship might come to an end? (2) Do you have any idea whether, for each of you, this is your first partner? (3) How attached are you to each other's family?

If they can see any way the relationship might be ended, short of death, they are not well bonded, and I would not work at this time toward setting a wedding date. I would, however, urge them to break up and not date at all for at least six months and to work through the guilt and grief of the inappropriate intimacy. The second question frequently provokes inner reflection and sets an agenda that often has not occurred to the less experienced partner. Depending on how they resolve the discovery that one of the partners has been previously intimate, the relationship is very likely to end, at which time both need time and space for grief. The question about their families is critical. Where parents are already "bonding" to their child's lover, there are excellent prospects for seeing the family surround the newly bonding pair in all of the ways they need. Humans are nicely equipped to continue caring for the young through their nesting phase.

*Q: I notice you have not used the word* fornication *in any of this talk about sexual intimacy. What is it, and why don't you use it?*

A: You are right. I have presented normal and healthy patterns in bonding in this discussion. The New Testament word which gets translated "fornication" is *porneia.* It is a word we can apply to our society very easily. The feminine form, *porne,* means, simply "a woman for sale." The masculine form, *pornos,* means "a man for sale." Today's word *pornography* means "sexual stimulation for sale." You can see where the word has gone in our vocabulary. So, fornication refers to any sort of casual sex or sex for hire. But it also refers to the use of magazines or movies for sexual stimulation, since this uses other people's bodies in a trivial and cheap way.

Deuteronomy 22 describes many sexual crimes punishable by death, and in no case is the crime in any way determined by whether or not pregnancy occurred from the sexual encounter. The crime consisted of "trivializing" the sexual gift of bonding. In only one case was the death penalty suspended in Deuteronomy: if neither the man nor the woman was betrothed to another. In such a case, "he shall pay the girl's father fifty shekels of silver. He must marry the girl, for he has violated her. He can never divorce her as long as he lives."[6] The penalty appears to take notice of the likelihood of bonding, even under circumstances in which sexual contact was thought to be temporary and furtive. And it also notes the probability that sexual contact of any sort is likely to awaken an appetite that will run wild; hence, even for adultery he may not divorce her, not "for any reason." In the Old Testament, the term of sexual endearment is translated "to know." So, Adam "knew Eve" or Abraham "knew Sarah." This is the intimate knowledge of a mature bonding process. Two other terms are used which translate as "lying with" and "violated" or raped her. It remains only to ask, "Why is fornication sin?" It is clear that it is sin because it exploits both the one who initiates the casual intimacy and the one who is drawn into it. Our entire culture is pockmarked by deformed sexual appetites which were first awakened when a previously experienced predator—of either sex—seduced a relatively innocent one. We, like the society of the ancient Greeks to whom Paul was writing so often about the dangers of fornication, are a society of pornography and fornication. In this book, I am assuming that the readers join me in deploring that tragic social condition and that they also join me in working to recover the power and sanctity of sexual bonding.

Neither the Old Testament nor the New Testament has anything to say about premature bonding within the family-sanctioned arrangements which paved the way for legal marriage. None of the statements about fornication, either in Deuteronomy or in Paul, fits the untimely bonding which may have occurred then and certainly occurs now. The tragedy behind fornication and pornography is not that they involve sexual pleasure and intimacy, but that they are casual, trivial, and are viewed as a mere exchange of coins or friendship for pleasure. That is why the warning in Revelation classifies the *porneia* people with "magic arts," and with "the murderers, the idolaters and everyone who loves and practices falsehood." These are all guaranteed eternal damnation.

In the famous Kinsey studies of twelve thousand males (published in 1948) it was surprising to find that "religion" was not as significant a difference in classifying sexual behavior as was "educational level." Casual sexual contact between the sexes was much more common among males of the lower educational levels than among other higher educated groups. Thus, fornication or the casual sex of *porneia* was more likely among the lower educational groups in Kinsey's studies.[7] Today, with massive media blitz and with widespread mixing of the adolescent population in high schools and universities, the former lower-educational class sexual patterns appear to be more pervasive than ever at all levels of society. Remember that the entrance of God's word brings light, and where there is no light there often appears to be no sensitivity to sin. But while the so-called happy heathen appear to go about their casual sex without conscience, they are not free to escape the consequences: a ripping of the dream of one exclusive pleasure and an intimacy relationship that will last forever.

When Bill heard me speak on pair bonding in his church, he asked me very quietly afterward why God had not sent me just one week earlier. "I had intercourse with my girl friend only this week, and I would never have done it if I had known how God wanted it to be."

More typically, we encounter those who have moved along for a short time in the fast lane during high school and formed their first bonds simply out of a desire to conform to the popular culture as they understood it. "I wonder whether I will ever be able to erase the feelings that I will always want Monty," Beverly wept during the private premarital counseling session she had scheduled before I met with her and the Christian man to whom she was now engaged. We must never imagine that the term *fornication* is merely a label for our own convenience. It is the name of a major crime against the image of God. So, *porneia* is anti-Christ in an ultimate and final sense. And I must say that I rarely meet among our young any who are immoral or fornicators. More often, those who weep with me are concerned about a relationship which has been splendid, but is moving faster than they can control. No doubt the Holy Spirit, in inspiring Holy Scripture, sensed that the faith community would find ways to rescue the victims of bonding passion, without needing to dictate the formal rules to parallel those for the *porneia* people.

*Q: Can a person be double-bonded, that is, can you bond with two people at the same time, or over time? What if you were once bonded sexually, say before you were married?*

A: In the next chapter I will want to discuss some of these issues. But the answer is yes, you can be double-bonded. And it is common for the first bond to haunt all future relationships. I will suggest ways to recover from the power of a lost bond. Ultimately, humans are able to choose and to control the direction their bonding will go, and that capacity is surely a significant part of what it is to be human. *Agape* love is not, as many theologians would have you think, simply a heightened form of love; *agape* is "targeted affection" in which the person deliberately chooses whom to love. This is why only *agape* can be commanded. All other loves, *eros, philia,* and *storge,* are spontaneous and situated in the context of particular relationships. But we will look at alien bonding, broken bonds, and recovery from lost bonds in chapter four.

*Q: Where does full-body hugging fit in the pair-bonding steps?*

A: It is important to remember that early pair bonding and friendship bonding are very similar. We will retain strong friendship bonds for a lifetime and they will never become *eros*-based or genital. They are held at a neutral point by the fact that most of them are *storge*-based, or "familial" in nature. Notice how you pat your friends on the back as you embrace them. This is the maternal/paternal signal that the relationship you cherish is based in mutual concern which is "like a member of the family." The full-body embrace tends not to appear in a friendship bond until the equivalent of bonding step seven is reached. If it does, then it has been a part of the instant-intimacy gimmick used by social climbers. Watch what happens to the faces in the full-body embrace. They must move to the cheek-to-cheek position or to an intimate kissing position.

This brings on step eight, intimacies to the head. So, even without targeting the action, you find yourself in a position to brush the neck with your lips. But the full-body embrace, Morris notes, also occurs among nonamorous adults at times of great tragedy or ecstasy. Morris believes this is a return to "infancy" and the need to hold and be held. At any rate, it is important to observe that not all hugging is grounded in the pair-bonding sequence. Morris also suggests that you watch nonamorous adult embraces. Note the frequency with which patting behavior is included. It is as if to remind ourselves that this is a nonsexual encounter. The patting on the back, the hand, or the face may be rooted in the parent-child relationship. It may well be that these gestures are our ways of differentiating between pair-bonding behavior and more fundamental social behavior within our species.

*Q: In Christian circles there appear to be several of these early steps in pair bonding in use between the "brothers and sisters." What does this do to the pair-bonding theory?*
**A:** There is an incest taboo that tends to defuse contact between members of a family and between people in the family of God, if all other circumstances are healthy. There is common closeness between members of a family and those of the family of God, when all other circumstances are healthy. There is common acceptance of eye contact, touch, embrace, and kiss within the natural family or the family of God, but only if it is done in the presence of the witnessing family. The incest taboo will instinctually trigger a sense of embarrassment and impropriety if the gestures occur without those witnesses; the gestures are then known to be ambiguous and therefore dishonest. Your question opens the door to the issue of sexual failure within the Christian community. The spiritual counselor stands in a unique relationship to the "brother or sister" in need. There is a high vulnerability to sexual seduction when the spiritual agenda is open or any agenda is related to affective/ emotional hurt or grief. And the priest/minister or other confidant is gifted with empathy. Otherwise there would not be time or priority for the caring listening. In these circumstances both counselor and client are highly vulnera-

ble to switching to pair-bonding steps, if eyes, touch, or embrace are used. The absolute privacy of the home or the counseling office is another of those potentially destructive settings because it predicts absolute intimacy. So, in the community of faith, absolute privacy is modified by the planned controls of glass paneled doors, telephone checks, physical distancing during conversation, and even the neutralizing effects of photographs of the pastor's spouse and family that stand between the two persons as witnesses.

Dr. Ira Gallaway, mature and experienced pastor, once advised our seminary seniors to train a cadre of gentle and wise women to whom to refer women who needed more than anything else to be held and cradled while they wept. "You cannot do it," he told them, "but many women whose hearts are broken need to be held." The opposite would be true for women counseling men. If the physical embrace is introduced in a private setting, it automatically triggers the pair bonding patterning, and the incest taboo has vanished. A similar violation of the incest taboo occurs in the small nuclear family which determines to "be a family" and to exclude the world by extended vacations, trips, and travel. The incest rate tends to skyrocket, likely because there are not enough "witnesses" to sustain the incest taboo. If the family included a half-dozen children, there would never be absolute privacy for inappropriate intimacy and the triggering of the bonding steps.

*wrong*

If the teens in your church are not much inclined to date each other, but seem predictably to reach out to develop social contact with other equally high-quality young people from other faith communities, the incest taboo may help you to understand their patterns of dating.

*Q: Are the pair-bonding steps an early warning signal that an adulterous or alien bond might be forming?*

**A:** If we could read them, they would serve as such a warning. However, since we use the same signals to identify friends, we are often quite unaware that an inappropriate bond is under way. It is important to keep in mind the public-versus-private checkpoint above. We will get the warning signal clearly if we move to privacy, to scheduled and secretive meeting points. The steps in seduction must also run over the same blueprint as those to holy ecstasy. James wrote: "When tempted, no one should say, 'God is tempting me.' For God cannot be tempted by evil, nor does he tempt anyone; but each one is tempted when, by his own evil desire, he is dragged away and enticed. Then, after desire has conceived, it gives birth to sin; and sin, when it is full-grown, gives birth to death" (James 1:13–15).

*Q: Does pair bonding apply to homosexual relationships?*
*A:* No doubt the steps would be the same between two persons of the same sex. The incest taboo controls most of these possibilities. However, exploratory sexual contact does occur for most children, and if this occurs with the same sex and runs into adolescence, it tends to form an affectional bond. Most of this exploratory contact is distinctly heterosexual, as study of conversations and thoughts of the children and adolescents will verify. The contact is anticipatory of future heterosexual experience. When this is the case, it is not homosexual in any real sense, and the relationships that may have been established will break away as heterosexual dating becomes a possibility.

Where a male-to-male targeting or a female-to-female bonding develops, the early experience will tend to follow the pair-bonding sequence. But the male homosexual experience, once the first significant bond breaks, tends to be almost instantly and perpetually focused on genital contact. The lesbian experience, for reasons that have to do with female sexuality and affectional gifts, is generally less promiscuous, but neither the homosexual nor the lesbian bond tends to hold. *The Bond That Breaks . . .* is the title of an important book on homosexuality. Another, *Homosexuality: A Symbolic Confusion,*[8] points to, but does not significantly develop the idea that the image of God, male and female requires that both be bonded together to represent God's presence and work in the world. If that is true, then deliberate targeting of affection to form "one flesh" of two males or two females constitutes blasphemy against the divine image, calling the partial "whole," which constitutes labeling Creation's "good" as "evil."

# 4

## What Has Gone Wrong with the Bonding?

△

I now remember that I had caught an image of her from my peripheral vision as she kept moving to the back of the line of people responding to my seminar on pair bonding. Several hundred teens had cheered me on as I put Scripture and human development together as a blueprint for holy living. At last, the woman, who was now at the end of the line, opened her mouth to speak. But instead she burst into tears.

When she could finally begin to talk, this was her story: "You have no idea what this seminar did for me. Only this week my pastor told me I should file for divorce. Daniel keeps an apartment in the city where he is on call all week. I have learned that he is sharing it with another woman. I don't know what to do."

I was glad she had waited until the teens had drifted on to the next coliseum event, since Polly would have embarrassed herself in front of them. I said, "I can't imagine anyone telling you to file for divorce when you are so clearly still deeply attached to Daniel. Are you aware how strongly you are committed to him?"

"I know," Polly answered, as she drew out a recent photograph of their family of five. A graduate, she told me, of a top Christian university, Daniel had served on the *Campus Life* staff on the West Coast, but he came home one evening to say that he did not believe in God any more and was resigning. It turned out that he had become sexually involved outside the marriage, then, too. The present case was the second affair of which Polly was aware.

I was booked in the major city where they lived and found myself, within the week, sitting in their home. They had completed the Myers-Briggs personality inventories to give me some insight into how they viewed the world. When I was alone with Dan, he reconstructed his history. "I was saved in a back-yard Bible school," he volunteered, "or at least my mother tells me I was. I don't think I ever was a Christian." He told of growing up in a Bible church, of being youth group president. Then he told of "double-facing" his high school years. He was president of his church youth group with high visibility there and was also having regular intercourse with his girl friend. Meeting Polly at the university, he sensed he would have to "wait," so pursued a fairly quick marriage.

Three years after I met Polly and Dan, Dan was into yet another live-in relationship. Polly had left the state and had begun litigation to gain financial assistance with the children. She was beginning to rebuild her life. Two weeks before the automatic no-fault divorce would become final, I had a call, then a visit from Dan. He drove the three-state span, and for two hours he explored the alternatives still open to him. He weighed his attachments. "Go home," I suggested, "and try to write your 'last letter' to the live-in girl friend. And if for some reason you cannot bring yourself to write it, try writing one to Polly and the children. Try telling them good-bye and why. Then bring in the letter and let's weigh your decision."

When Dan was gone, the pool of tears on the floor in front of his chair was a profound testimony to the absolute agony experienced by a person who has walked into a morass of tangled and deformed bonds. He has never returned. The cost was very great and has left a half-dozen people emotionally bankrupt, having to start over again in building trust and then risking the loss of affection.

In this chapter I want to examine the patterns and effects of broken bonds. It will then be important to see the roots and the impact that comes from an alien bond which is introduced into a monogamous bond. To begin to understand how tangled bonding occurs, we will need to examine what has gone wrong with the Creation, and to discover a fault line that extends further than the human family. Finally, I want to open the subject of how one might recover from straying into alien bonding and to outline the recovery trajectory that brings a person back from the tragedy of a broken bond.

## The Broken Bond

For every broken bond there is at least one broken heart. Often there are many. Jesus sensed this when he responded to the question of whether a man might divorce a woman for "any and every reason." Look at it in Matthew 19. Jesus finds the question to be so insulting to human values that he refuses to answer the question. Instead, he takes them back to the primer, to the lesson: "For this reason a man will leave his father and mother and be united to his wife, and the two of them will become one flesh." To this Genesis 2 foundation, he then adds the cry: "So they are no longer two, but one. Therefore what God has joined together, let man not separate" (Matt. 19:5–6).

Still the heckling Pharisees were not satisfied. "Why then," they asked, "did Moses command that a man give his wife a certificate of divorce and send her away?" (v. 7).

Jesus replied, "Moses permitted you to divorce your wives because your hearts were hard. But it was not this way from the beginning. I tell you that anyone who divorces his wife and marries another woman commits adultery" (vv. 8–9).

We have most often read Jesus on divorce and missed the role adultery plays. Adultery is the primary universal acid which leaves the double effect of (1) destroying the pair bond; and (2) hardening the heart of one or both of the persons.

Those of us who devoutly read the Bible tend to study Jesus on the subject with a preoccupation for finding the loophole or the "grounds for divorce" in his words. When we do that, we are indulging in exactly the sort of legalism the Pharisees were using on Jesus. We are not likely to keep faith with the words of Jesus unless we study his actions and regard them as commentary on his words. Consider how blind we have been to his treatment of the much-divorced "woman at the well" of John 4. If we took the trouble to reconcile his words with his actions we would have an immediate rebuke on our preoccupation with making rules to cover every circumstance. Jesus simply will not get embroiled in the legal/civil aspects of marriage or divorce. Instead, Jesus reads hearts and treasures persons. He also is fanatical about working with the present circumstance instead of demanding some inhumane return to idealism which, if it ever existed, is now well out of reach without destroying other innocent persons. Jesus is a "radical" in the sense that he goes for the root of every issue. He is amazingly able to focus on the universal value in every situation—the deeper principle behind the laws that have been invented to protect the value. In that spirit, I want to keep us focused on *persons* as the highest value of the Creation, and *sin* as both the original and the persistent destructive force and pattern which threatens life's most intimate relationships.

In our culture we may need to read Jesus' words upside down. He had to confront a culture in which men divorced women and put them on the street without shelter, money, or skill. Today, it is likely to be the woman who, at almost any whim, may "restrain" the man and put him out of the home, demand his money, and leave him obligated by the court to support two households. Given the double-edged possibilities in our culture, it is important that we look again at the issue Jesus wanted to get at when he expressed concern lest one of the persons, in breaking the bond, might "cause the other to commit adultery."

Tom married a young woman who desperately wanted to "get out of the house" at her family's home. No one suspected that she may have loved the escape more than she was attached to Tom. Within two years she invited her equally troubled sister to live with them. Then in a few months Tom's young wife had him "restrained" legally and put him out of the house, out of the marriage, and back into the single life he thought he had left.

Jesus no doubt intended to convey to us the idea that an unattached woman could not survive in that culture without tragic consequences in the wake of divorce. She had limited options in those days: (1) She could produce a meager income by entering public prostitution; (2) a near-relative with money could take her in as a domestic servant; or (3) a man of marginal reputation might marry her following her disgrace through divorce.

Today, although Tom and men like him have more options than a woman did in Jesus' day, a male is quite fragile and tends not to thrive as well as a woman when left alone. "For this cause shall a man leave" the security of home and "cleave to his wife" (Matt. 19:5 KJV) tells us something about who may really be the weaker sex. And given a man's need for sexual intimacy, the text, if spoken for today's audience, might have continued: "whoever causes her husband to commit adultery by putting him out of the house. . . ."

It becomes clear, then, that the first appropriate question for us to ask of anyone in a troubled relationship is: "How attached are you to your spouse?" All other questions become irrelevant until the strength of the bond is explored. And it becomes clear that a deeply bonded relationship can survive virtually anything. To suggest any concrete act or behavior as "grounds for divorce" may be near to blasphemy, since such an assertion may tell us more about the condition of the speaker's heart than it does about the possibilities that remain for the marriage in question. Pharisees and Egyptians, to name two groups from the two Testaments, are well known for their "hardness of heart." But theirs are not so hard as the hearts of those who quickly leap to break asunder what God has joined together.

The "hardened heart" most often results from establishing an alien bond. It is not uncommon for an unfaithful spouse to lose interest in intimacy with the spouse. Bill became aloof from Jan several months before she was aware that there was someone else. Looking back, she can now recall some irregular patterns of evening "business" that took Bill away mysteriously. But the sexual intimacy ended between Bill and Jan just before Bill and his illicit lover became sexually intimate. A built-in sense of monogamy commonly shuts down affectional feelings for the former lover. It is hard to think of this gift as one of monogamy when infidelity is brewing, yet the Creation vision and inclination is strong. A recent *Playboy* study which was never published found most men to be "square," preferring one woman to the many "bunnies" idealized by Playboy philosophy.[1]

The abandoned lover has a tendency, though normally at a lagging rate, to experience a hardening of affection toward the straying spouse. In cases where the affair is discovered and attacked, the strength of the bond may show itself in an angry assault, calculated to destroy the alien bond and to return the spouse to sanity and to the original bond. The assault is an index to the strength of the existing bond, although the words or actions hardly seem affectionate. Mary traced her husband's car to the duplex occupied by a suspected alien woman. When she could get no one to the door, she heaved a brick through a plate glass window, which brought her husband to the window in his underwear. It is not surprising that such an encounter, while motivated by a frantic desire to protect the marital bond, tends to strengthen the alien bond and to further shut down the husband's bond to the wife.

A slower death to the bond tends to occur when the offended spouse simply experiences the decline of affection in the marriage. In such cases, touch, eye contact, and higher intimacies tend to wane: the almost certain path to extinction in any bond. Should the abandoned spouse simply accept the realities of a superseding alien bond, there is a gradual deadening of affection. We will look at the typical detail in this process in the final section devoted to recovery from a broken bond.

## Alien Bonding

When we combine our larger needs for intimacy and a whole network of friends with our need for ultimate intimacy in an exclusive pair bond, we can see that we may be in for some tension between the two. We could wish that "marriages were made in heaven," and that only two people might ever be attracted to each other. But the simple fact is that in our search for significant relationships we begin with the same sorts of recognition and attraction in friendships as we initiate in our pair-bonding relationship.

We saw in chapter one how important it is for us to win and to maintain a hand-held trampoline of some twenty to thirty people. Because there is a certain amount of safety in numbers, any of those trampoline holders who moves into an exclusive and absorbing friendship is a potential alien bond for a previously committed person. Since we live in a harried, jam-packed culture, our needs for intimate friendships are very great. It is not uncommon to pick out one other couple from the sea of faces and focus most of our social energy on them. But alien bonding is an almost inevitable tendency in two-couple friendships. You have seen it happen. Sometimes there is a swap, but more often there is an emerging pair of new lovers and the remaining odd couple who have not entered into an alien bond—although sometimes they pair off out of desperation. Three or four couples who form an intentional cluster for social purposes provide the witnesses which we need to hold the incest taboo in place. Illicit pairing rarely occurs in such larger groups.

You can often detect when an alien bond has begun to form. The behavior is simple pair bonding, so the pattern is visible: the eye contact, the casual physical contact, the shared trivia, and eventually everything. In a similar way, professional counselors and ministers are trained to detect "transference" patterns by which the counselor is the object of a crush from the client or the parishioner. "Counter transference" refers to what happens when the counselor falls in love with the client. The words may help us describe a professional booby trap.

Pastor Jones listened as Jan described her unfulfilling marriage: "He never touches me anymore. I don't know what has happened. I don't feel wanted." Often the details are even more graphic, and the counselor or pastor may be evoked to feelings of pity, which turn easily into unrestrained pair bonding, and the client-counselor relationship has been tragically flawed. He might have said, "Is it all right if I give John a call? I want to talk with him." The pastor enjoys the unique position of being able to be a facilitator of what Creation and Redemption agree "ought to be," and thus is never the real "savior" at all.

It remains a simple axiom that pair bonding is under way (1) when significant investment of time focuses on the eyes and face; and (2) when sufficient privacy exists to shield gestures of touch. And no one is more vulnerable to sexual seduction than (3) when giving comfort, empathy, or feeling a sense of pity for the other person. This means that counselors are dealing daily, as a matter of vocation, with the highest-risk kinds of relationships complicated by the most seductive of content.

There is another way to harden the heart or break a bond. If a marriage is never consummated sexually, most societies offer annulment and the return of the virginal identity and name. But some marriages *are* consummated sexually, only to drop back to virtually no sexual communication in the marriage. When large samples indicate that the frequency of intercourse in North America stands at about three and one half times per week for married couples, a marriage in which intercourse occurs only two or three times every six months falls dangerously near the "celibacy" commitment line. Bob married Marge both because he was in love with her and because she was his best friend in every way. Once sexually active during high school, now Bob was a Christian, and he and Marge waited for marriage to consummate the bond sexually. Marge seemed warm enough, eager to be close. But once married, Bob learned that sexual intimacy was repugnant to Marge. She thought he was "an animal," and she began to ration the contact with "maybe" and conditional controls. Their total intercourse during the second year of marriage fell below ten encounters. "I was so angry," he said, "that I found myself wishing she would be killed in a traffic accident."

Bob and Marge have a partnership but not a bond. They

may survive as partners or roommates for a little longer, but marriages that are not sexually bonded tend not to last. The central tendency in any partnership is toward an adversary relationship. It becomes necessary to protect the partnership with a charter and rules governing almost every detail. A bonded marriage can survive unequal distribution of labor, unexplained behaviors, almost anything. But a partnership tends to explode. It is troublesome, but true, that you can often predict that a marriage is in trouble if you do not see significant signs that the pair bond is "alive and well." The apostle Paul makes the point explicitly, with every warning:

> The wife's body does not belong to her alone but also to her husband. In the same way, the husband's body does not belong to him alone but also to his wife. Do not deprive each other except by mutual consent and for a time, so that you may devote yourselves to prayer. Then come together again so that Satan will not tempt you because of your lack of self-control.
>
> 1 Corinthians 7:4–5

### Tournament Species

Melvin Konner thinks that humans fall into a pair-bonding class occupied by red-winged blackbirds and bank swallows. While they are clearly pair-bonding species, they are "equally clearly, imperfectly so." Konner is a biologist and anthropologist who first came to prominence while at Harvard, but he is now at Emory. In his *The Tangled Wing: Biological Constraints on the Human Spirit,* he places a major focus on pair bonding in humans compared to similar bonding within animal and bird species.[2]

Konner cites the work of other anthropologists to form the picture of human societies as mostly polygynous. In such societies one man may be married to two or more women. Of 849 human societies examined, 708 (83%) were polygynous to some degree. Of the 137 who were classified monogamous (16%), most included arrangements by which one might have a series of different spouses. Polyandry, in which one woman might have more than one husband, occurred in only four of the societies studied.

The potential solidarity in Creation which links humans, animals, and birds is established in Scripture. John Wesley saw it and treated it in his sermon commonly titled "The General Deliverance."[3] His original title for the sermon was "The Brute Creation." Dr. Timothy Smith, Nazarene historian from Johns Hopkins University, quipped in an Asbury chapel, "While I knew that John Wesley had a fondness for his horses and that he hoped to see them in heaven, I was unaware of his view that humans are linked together with animals both in the Creation and in the Fall." John Wesley, in that sermon, suggests that the whole Creation which is groaning for redemption will, in fact, one day be fully redeemed. At that point the animals will not only be restored to their original innocence, but will be elevated to a better estate. At any rate, "the lion will lie down with the lamb and a little child shall lead them." Dr. Smith expressed the concern that Creation science people might be troubled by John Wesley, but that what we need more than an isolated "textual" science is Creation theology, "and we could do worse than begin where John Wesley left off."

Melvin Konner shows no interest in pursuing Wesley's idea of such a Creation solidarity. But it may be that he illustrates that solidarity by his findings and by the way he organizes his evidence. As you work through his chapter entitled, of all things, "Lust," you will be struck by the fact that a witness remains in isolated species of birds and animals. There are in both sets those species which are monogamous and fiercely so. They comprise less than 15 percent of animals and birds. If you read the popular polls on human virginity at marriage and on fidelity within marriage, you will be astonished to find that the witness among humans follows a similar profile. By "witness" I mean the absolute fidelity to the image-of-God/male-and-female, which fanatically adheres to "one man plus one woman" forming the effective testimony to the nature and character of God. I unfolded this concept in chapter two.

Imperfectly bonding species of animals and birds have some common characteristics:

1. *Fierce competition.* The larger, dominant, more colorful or more "armed" sex competes for a harem and takes them for reproductive purposes. About 85 percent of animals and birds are organized around a larger, dominant male. He may have antlers, highly colored plumage, or other ornamentation. About 3 percent are organized around a larger, more ornamented, female, in which case the harem is a collection of males smaller than herself. She courts them, then feeds and protects them in exchange for sperm. The South African phalarope, a shorebird, is an example.

2. *Polygyny.* The imperfectly bonding species may gather a series of single mates, usually by the season, abandoning them at the end of the season with the launching of a set of young. Or the species is characterized by multiple matings of a seasonal or longer period, as with red-winged blackbirds. The red-wings, of course, are the males—and the male will gather as many females as he can reasonably feed. The single criterion seems to be the richness of his territory in a given season.

3. *Hierarchical structure.* The less than perfect model of the "family" for these species is a corporate model, arranged with the large dominant leader commandeering the weaker spouse(s), with the young well insulated and separated from the dominant boss.

4. *Low investment in the care of the young.* Here the characteristics of the less perfectly bonding species range all the way from "changing diapers is woman's work" to abuse and infanticide. Among the cats, both domestic and wild, the male is strongly inclined to kill the newborns. A clear division of labor, when it comes to care of the young, characterizes even the gentler of the imperfectly bonding dominant leaders.

The more perfectly bonding species of animals and birds throw even more light on our human patterns in intimate relationships. They tend to be characterized by:

1. *Similar size, ornamentation, and age at maturity.* The males and females mature at about the same calendar age. And they are not easily distinguished from each other on sight. There are no antlers or distinct colors to mark them

apart. They form what we often speak of as a "matched set."

2. *Non-competitive.* Evidently these species are content with some inner assurance that "there will be a mate for me if I wait." And there is. Whereas among the imperfectly bonding elephant seals, more than 85 percent of one herd of females was impregnated by only 4 percent of the males—leaving 96 percent of the males to compete for the remaining females—the more perfectly bonding species sing out, "To each its own!" There is no violence in the courting phase with these. I note that a puzzling pattern hangs over the Christian college campus: If a young woman is once seen in public with a young man, the other men who might have dated her tend to drop back and "punt," no doubt regretting that they did not move more quickly, but respecting the right of the leading male. The frustration may be more easily handled if it is seen as a characteristic of more perfectly bonding males. In some less gentle communities there might be blood on the gymnasium floor to determine who took her out on the second date.

3. *Non-hierarchical.* In these pairs, there is no need to elect a chairperson for the committee of two. Instead, there is cooperation, mutual respect, and consensus. There is high communication, because the bond drives them to move, to hunt, to nest, and to live out their lives in an adventure for two. The tiny marmoset monkeys of South America bond for life. Their young typically come in sets of twins. The male carries the helpless young most of the time, releasing them to the mother only for feeding. By this arrangement, the family is always together.

4. *Long, elaborate courtship.* The African ringdove carries out an extended gesturing, posturing ritual. The male brain, whose testosterone production is triggered by spring sunlight, activates the stretching, swooning gesturing toward the female. She watches, unmoved for some time, then begins to mirror his movement. A domestic version, the lovebird pairs in the pet shop, must always be kept in pairs, and entertain the owners by this extended courting behavior. Researchers have found that the female's lutenizing hormones are not affected by sunlight, but that they

are aroused by watching the lovesick gestures of the male. The female's hormones are essential in preparing her for breeding and egg production. Experiments have shown that the female ringdove will respond to a movie of a male ringdove going through his courting ritual, and her hormones will be released, triggering her courting mirror responses.

5. *Nest-building ahead of breeding.* The courtship—which culminates, seasonally, in mating—is not consummated until the nest is built. It is commonly a joint project. The male ringdove brings the twigs; the female positions herself at the nesting site and arranges the building materials around her own body to form the nest. Once breeding occurs, the ringdoves trade off in about equal time investment to sit on the eggs until they hatch.

6. *High investment in the care of the young.* Here the witness is perhaps most profound. The male ringdove is equipped with "crop milk" production matching that of the female, so that both father and mother may feed the young from the open mouth. The marmoset monkeys illustrate the more mobile types. Other of the pair-bonding species characterized by high investment in the care of the young by the male include the gibbons, bat-eared foxes, and coyotes.

It is not appropriate, of course, to apply the biology and the instinctual patterns of animals and birds to humans. But it may be helpful to use those pair-bonding patterns as analogies for human behavior we observe every day all around us. And it does become plausible to speculate that the Fall in Genesis 3 may be most visible on this planet in the deformed bonding patterns that extend throughout the vertebrate species. We have danced all sorts of patterns around the first three chapters of Genesis, trying to divert attention from issues of sex, nudity, and reproduction. Since Holy Scripture, outside of the obviously obscure "coded secret messages" of the Book of Revelation, tends to speak plainly, it should not be surprising if the Genesis material were found to be straightforward. At the moment, I cannot imagine a more profound frustration for the millions of human, animal, and bird species on this planet than for pair bonding to be turned into a flawed aspect of life. Bound to reproductive obligation as we are, bonding of some sort, even though it is deformed, seems inescapable. And, for humans, we are locked in to sexual pleasure as a significant affirmation of personal worth and as an appetite that draws fuel and energy from its expression. It is difficult to imagine a more tragic seduction than one that would have collapsed our own pleasure and reproductive protection, and, in the same act, to have collapsed the domestic security of most other species of vertebrates. We have turned ourselves into adversaries and carnivores and introduced violence across all warm-blooded layers of the life chain, until history is, indeed, written red in tooth and claw. Violence, as any Freudian psychologist will tell you, is clearly the "flip side" of affection. The homicide statistics in any year tell the story. Typically, more than 90 percent of all murders involve one member of the family murdering another. Jesse Jackson cries out for all of us when he warns that it is not our enemies who kill us, but "brothers kill brothers." His text, of course, comes from Genesis, and the prototypes are Cain and Abel.

## Recovery from Broken Bonding

The birds and animals await the "general deliverance" when Jesus returns to restore the new heavens and the new earth. John Wesley saw that day and rejoiced for the animals. But what about humans and the central tendency in large numbers of us toward imperfect bonding? What is it that causes our young to dread marriage because "we don't know any married people who are in love"? And, indeed, why does the magic go out for so many pairs after the honeymoon?

Pair bonding, which takes thousands of hours of investment in the early months of a relationship, requires a continuing and extensive stoking of the fires. This means that lovers must continue to behave like lovers, beginning with the first bonding step and working up the entire ladder, for a lifetime. On the phone Linda told me that she and her husband had been separated twice during the past year, and that while they were now back together, she was not optimistic that they could continue in such a cold, trucelike living arrangement. I commented, "I expect you need to begin again at step one with him. Do the two of you look into each other's eyes when you are talking to each other?"

"I can't remember how long ago it has been since we looked at each other while we were talking," she replied. "We make it a point, I think, to look away when we speak. I still find myself stealing glimpses of George when he doesn't know it. But if he looks up, I look away." I asked Linda whether she recognized where that placed them on the pair bonding scale. She did.

"You will have to go back and start over," I told her, "and that could recapture the 'romance' you have lost, too. Think how lonely your husband must feel. It takes only one person to start over again. See whether you feel any positive excitement at the sight of him coming up the walk. If you do, you can recapture the magic. But it will take time, eye contact, and touch. If you are not now looking into his eyes, it means you do not have an honest relationship. Start telling him the truth across the table and look him right in the face while you tell him something like this: 'George, I used to love you so much that I'm spoiled for this world if we can't recapture it again.' " The eyes are the window of the soul, and eye contact goes out of any relationship that contains dishonesty in it. Recovery requires a return to honesty, and even a small piece of honesty such as what I suggested to Linda is enough to begin. The larger chunks of honesty can come later.

*eye contact*

The pair bond needs periodic rejuvenation. Fasting is a well-known practice used to stimulate health in the body's digestive system and general well-being. A couple needs occasional, perhaps regular, interruption of intimacy to stimulate appreciation for it. Old Testament laws about purification guaranteed that a man could not even touch his wife except in two-week intervals. She was technically "unclean" during the menses and for several days afterward. This meant that devout Jews were recycled every month to begin all over again with eye-to-body, eye-to-eye, and voice-to-voice limits. This guarantees high stimulation of desire and helps us to understand the sexual vitality of some very aged people. It is standard practice in one Roman-Catholic-based program in sex therapy to separate the couple and forbid intimacy for several days in a retreat setting. During that time, the therapy consists largely of face-to-face conversation exercises. These are supplemented on about the third day by hand-to-face contact during conversation. It is typical that sexual arousal and healing of both impotence and frigidity occur following such a therapy sequence. It is comic, perhaps, that we now have to purchase as therapy the very experiences which we are programmed to give ourselves, if we would only turn off the television and begin again to speak to each other and to listen with interest and empathy.

## Recovery Following the Loss of a Bond

We instinctually expect a spouse to pass through a grief-and-healing period following the loss of a partner through death. Most cultures have a specified or unspoken traditional mourning period. But in North America we have not yet ritualized the same expectations for persons who have experienced the loss of a significant intimate bond. It is my observation that Elizabeth Kubler-Ross has served us well in her studies of "death and dying" and of the grief process, and that these ideas apply in a most useful way when people close to us have to deal with a bond that is terminated either by death or by other causes.[4] When Denise told me that Dallas had broken their engagement, my first impulse was to "fix her up" with one of my students who was both eligible and lonely. But her intuitions were wiser than mine when she said she would like to meet him, "But I don't think I will be ready to date anyone for a while yet." Look at the stair steps out of grief, summarized here from Kubler-Ross:

ACCEPTANCE
DEPRESSION
BARGAINING

ANGER

DENIAL

For each of these stages in grieving, I want to play out some scenarios or lines I have heard. It is my observation that grieving takes a lot of time, and there is a yo-yo effect by which a person who has worked all the way up to acceptance may have a sudden flashback to denial or anger or bargaining. With each descent into the pit, it is necessary to work the way back up. While we are never entirely free of the memory of an old and treasured relationship, and any fragment of that memory may trigger the descent to the bottom of the abyss, both the *frequency* and the *power* of that memory tend to become mellow if the grieving process includes the elements we will see in the acceptance stage.

1. *Denial.* "I never loved him anyway." Or, more commonly, as the bond is disintegrating: "We never should have married; I was never in love with her." Denial is the first insulating device that humans use. It often saves one's sanity. Psychosis and long-term mental illness is a fixed state of denial of reality, but we all begin to use it as an anesthetic to our terrible hurt at the first sense of loss. You can see that denial prevents healing from ever progressing. It shows up in a marital spat: "What did I do?" "Oh, it was nothing!" "Nothing? And you are acting like that?" "Nothing! I said it was nothing!" "Oh, nothing. I'm so glad it was nothing. I thought it was something!" No progress can be made in a standoff from truth. It marks significant progress when the grief moves on to step two.

2. *Anger.* "I could kill him for making a fool of me." Or, "I'll never trust another woman, not after she wrapped me around her little finger, then brushed me off, no sir!" These are blurred pieces of angry talk, but anger, as it gets expressed, tends to become more articulate. I once asked Richard to write out "an open letter to Sharon." In it he began with expressions that were both violent and obscene. "Don't mail it," I said, "but I want to read the pages and discuss them with you." In six months Richard had written some six hundred pages of anger, but the last two hundred or so were tinted with steps three through five. At last, he became a very mellow minister who is nicely equipped to deal with almost any sort of grief his people may be experiencing.

3. *Bargaining.* "God, if you care anything about me, bring him back into my life. I want him at any cost." Or,

"I'll show her she is not the only fish in the puddle." You can see that the first three steps are blindly self-centered. They also leave a person most vulnerable to substituting a new relationship for the lost one. Alliances made during these early stages of grief are almost certain to pick up the freight of the lost bond. Imagine marrying someone who was trying to prove his or her acceptability to someone else in order to make a big point to the previous spouse or lover.

4. *Depression.* "I'm not worth loving. No one will ever come into my life again." Or, "My life has ended." Or again, "Life as I have known it on this planet has ended." While these sound desperate—and a trusted confidant must read these cues with an eye to seeing the depressed person through a potential trough of self-destructive thoughts—depression is essential to recovery from grief. These negative thoughts are the first breakthrough to the "world of others." It is the first sign of deliverance from pure self-centeredness. Although self-centeredness is essential to survival, it is destructive on a wide scale in social relationships. And a new and healthy relationship will require that the vantage point take in the social, other-persons perspective. Depression is the negative, self-depreciating end of final healing. All of us, as we are delivered from absorbing self-centeredness must be able to renounce the "self" in a deliberate way. Depression needs understanding, and affirmation from a few close and trusted friends. Dependency on drugs or alcohol in moving through grief and the loss of a bond almost certainly delays healthy closure and healing.

5. *Acceptance.* "I thought for a while that I would never smile again." Or, "I will always be in debt to her. She taught me so much about myself!" Or again, "I wouldn't want it to happen to anybody, ever! But I am a better person for having walked through that dark valley. I hope he survived and will live again. After what has happened to me, it's not impossible that he may become a good and whole person, too." As with grief, the healing means that the old images and memories are contained. It is no longer necessary to deny the reality of the hurt, because "something beautiful, something good" has grown up in the ruins of the lost relationship.

It is easy to see that in the long run, the really healthy people you know have broken through to acceptance and have made it a way of life. They have left no sealed-off, forgotten closet in memory. They are not dragging around a clattering cadaver to haunt themselves or other people. Instead, their faces are the harvest of an honest approach to life, and other people who are passing through the same dark valley somehow detect that "here is a person who would understand and not criticize me."

There is no time table for recovery, but it is almost never rapid. Here are questions worth posing:

• How long did the bond take to develop to the point at which it broke?

• Would you imagine that your healing will occur more quickly than the original bonding?

• What have you done with all of the memorabilia you accumulated—the gifts, the pictures, the special memories?

• How have you gotten your own private peace that "this relationship will never live again"?

• Have you any assurance that the other person has completely closed the other end of the bond?

• Should you write a personal "letter to myself" to detail how you are closing down your affection and giving the tragedy over to God's grace?

Given the wide ramifications of total healing, the best rule is simply: Make no effort at paired social life until the yo-yo is under control, the grief has turned mellow through acceptance, and you are able to take the first steps toward another bond without the impulse to race to the top of the stairs.

## The Ultimate Cure for Defective Bonding

In this chapter, I have explored the terrain of tragic broken bonds. A broken bond, whether premature, marital, or alien, represents broken human aspirations. Living as we do in a fallen world, some of our best dreams get smashed or do not materialize as we hoped they would. But God has not left us without hope or without a remedy for all of the misadventures in human pair bonding.

The Old Testament amazingly ends with a word of hope

that strikes to the heart of the frustrations and the broken dreams of the human family. The doctrine of Creation opens with the ideal of "one woman and one man," and these form "one flesh, naked and unashamed." Yet much of history has been flawed since the Fall, and, as Melvin Konner notes, that history is marked by polygyny, polyandry, and tragic serial monogamy. It seems rarely marked by high fidelity and exclusive monogamy. Yet there is always hope: "When Elijah comes . . ." and "When Messiah comes . . ." were two phrases that were often on the lips of frustrated Israelites. They were most often "fantastic" phrases, and were not literally spoken in the hope of immediate deliverance. Many Christians today speak of "When Jesus comes . . ." but they would be quite surprised if Jesus were suddenly to appear or if they were suddenly struck dead and found themselves in the presence of the Lord. But the Old Testament ends on a note of absolute prophecy, specifically targeted at correcting the defective pair bonding that has plagued the human race so tragically since Genesis 3:

> "Surely the day is coming; it will burn like a furnace. All the arrogant and every evildoer will be stubble, and that day that is coming will set them on fire," says the Lord Almighty. "Not a root or a branch will be left to them. But for you who revere my name, the sun of righteousness will rise with healing in its wings. And you will go out and leap like calves released from the stall. Then you will trample down the wicked; they will be ashes under the soles of your feet on the day when I do these things," says the Lord Almighty.
> "Remember the law of my servant Moses, the decrees and laws I gave him at Horeb for all Israel.
> "See, I will send you the prophet Elijah before that great and dreadful day of the Lord comes. He will turn the hearts of the fathers to their children, and the hearts of the children to their fathers; or else I will come and strike the land with a curse."
>
> Malachi 4:1–6

The "word of the Lord" to Malachi puts the finger on the single most critical of the pair-bonding test points: a high investment in the care of the young. Males will be tamed. No longer will they regard women as chattel and children as property. And the "hardness of heart" which forced Moses to tolerate laws permitting divorce will be replaced by a mysterious healing of the wandering and hardening hearts. Their hearts will be turned with attachment and parental bonding to their children, just as children will be bonded to their fathers.

We are not left to imagine how this change will come about. In the amazing angelic words to Zechariah announcing the birth of John the Baptist, "Elijah" becomes tangible and present:[5]

"Do not be afraid, Zechariah; your prayer has been heard. Your wife Elizabeth will bear you a son, and you are to give him the name John. He will be a joy and delight to you, and many will rejoice because of his birth, for he will be great in the sight of the Lord. He is never to take wine or other fermented drink, and he will be filled with the Holy Spirit even from birth. Many of the people of Israel will he bring back to the Lord their God. And he will go on before the Lord, in the spirit and power of Elijah, to turn the hearts of the fathers to their children and the disobedient to the wisdom of the righteous—to make ready a people prepared for the Lord."

Both Elijah and John the Baptist are models of tough-minded, activist males. Neither might look quite right nestled into the typical Sunday morning passive worship service at your church. Yet both were God's special instruments, and both were marked by a delicate sensitivity to preserving and improving the quality of human life. So, how were the hearts of men to be "turned to their children"?

*Repentance* is the key. The word *repent* means, literally, "to come home," back where you belong in the universal sentiment of frustrated, failing, and broken-bonded humanity. Listen to John the Baptist's preaching:

". . . 'Prepare the way for the Lord,
    make straight paths for him. . . .
Every valley shall be filled in,
    every mountain and hill made low.

The crooked roads shall become straight,
the rough ways smooth.
And all mankind will see God's salvation.'. . .

[John said:] "You brood of vipers! Who warned you to flee from the coming wrath? Produce fruit in keeping with repentance. And do not begin to say to yourselves, 'We have Abraham as our father.' For I tell you that out of these stones God can raise up children for Abraham. . . ."

"What should we do then?"

John answered, "The man with two tunics should share with him who has none, and the one who has food should do the same."

Tax collectors also came to be baptized. "Teacher," they asked, "what should we do?"

"Don't collect any more than you are required to," he told them.

Then some soldiers asked him, "And what should we do?"

"Don't extort money and don't accuse people falsely—be content with your pay."

". . . I baptize you with water. But one more powerful than I will come, the thongs of whose sandals I am not worthy to untie. He will baptize you with the Holy Spirit and with fire. His winnowing fork is in his hand to clear his threshing floor and to gather the wheat into his barn, but he will burn up the chaff with unquenchable fire."

Luke 3:4–17

It becomes clear that repentance, coming home to the true yearnings of the human heart, requires obedience to God. That obedience may come as a result of a choice to obey, but God has enabled that choice in a special intervention by giving us Jesus. Jesus provides the Holy Spirit; the Holy Spirit is the cleansing agent who purifies our affections. The end result is that the hearts of the parents are turned to the children and the hearts of the children are turned to their fathers.

We sometimes feel helpless in the face of wayward "love" and destructive, alien bonding. The Greeks had many more words for love than we have in English. *Storge* spoke of spontaneous, inevitable feelings of loyalty that exist mutually between parent and child. *Philia* spoke of spontaneous, reciprocal feelings of warmth between friends. *Eros* spoke of spontaneous "desire" or "worship." But *agape* spoke of "targeted affection," as love under the deliberate control of one's will. "I kiss my young daughter because I love her," my colleague reported to me, expressing the *storge* attachment. "But I also kiss her in order to love her." What we know about pair bonding tells us that humans are uniquely in control of their affection. Repentance always carries with it the return-by-deliberate-choice, and with that coming home, the *bringing home* of one's affection.

Many of us rejoice that this "taming of the fathers" and turning of hearts to the familial bond is occurring on a large scale. We applaud the many practices which open the door to both parents' having more significant contact with the pregnancy and the delivery of their young. We applaud revised sex typing which enlarges options for both women and men, opening the door for active father care for the growing child. The trend has reached such proportions that now, for the first time, solid research evidence indicates that many junior-high children rate their parents as their best friends and best source of knowledge. And parents, independently, report high attachment and good relationships with their young teenagers. Many of us expect the Elijah trend to accelerate. And we rejoice!

## QUESTIONS PEOPLE ASK

*Q: I've seen couples who I know were intimate long before they were married, so I assume they were "bonded" as you call it. Yet it seemed as if getting married only started their troubles, and they divorced within a couple of years. How do you account for that?*

A: Many of our young are forming the idea that sexual pleasure without responsibility is the golden dream of adulthood. Our media content gives them the idea, of course, but so does teenage intercourse without fear of pregnancy or, at the worst, with the easy availability of abortion, if all else fails. Yet sexual pleasure is designed in the Creation to bond humans in the midst of full adult responsibility.

It is the Creation tranquilizer that makes parenthood, bill paying, and work tolerable. So couples who begin their intimacy without full responsibility for adult kinds of consequences have bought into a plastic dream. Legal marriage, meeting payments that are due, buying property, and knowing that you are responsible for other people in some final sense must seem very confining. You can see how they might long for the Hollywood fantasy of sex without responsibility. Such people are likely to be unhappy all of their lives. Compare them with those who laminated together their pleasure and their total adult responsibility package, and you will see how Creation was intended to work.

*Q: How can we protect our bond? There are so many alien bonders out there trying to break the marriage bonds.*

A: You are right. We live in a booby-trapped world. The very best insurance for your marital bond is to invest in the bonding process every day—significantly. If you are gazing into each other's eyes, holding each other for a few minutes on arrival and on departure, and running the ladder all the way to twelve on a mutually satisfying frequency, there is not likely to be anyone "out there" who can seduce either you or your spouse. The incest taboo to which I have referred is extended to the entire human race where an exclusive pair bond is thriving. Lust cannot take root, because all other persons are seen as sexual, yet deserving of the kind of exclusive, lifelong attachment they need, which means, "It will have to be somebody else!"

# 5

# Conception: Differentiating the "Adam"

△

"Oh! It's a boy!" she sobbed, bursting into tears. We watched on the sound home-movie film. It was the delivery room documentary of the birth of Justin Michael Brooks Joy. Every birth is special, and our clan is the richer for prenatal classes and well-trained fathers who served as "labor coaches." But Justin's birth was a blue-ribbon event. He was the first to be born after Grandpa learned about "birth bonding" and passed the good news along in time for his parents, Mike and Dorian, to get the physician's help in guaranteeing extra bonding time if the delivery went well.

The really big deal about Justin, however, was that he was the critical balance in the clan. Our grandchildren came like this: Jason, Heather, Jami, Lesli, Jordan—then Justin. The balance of boys to girls was loaded toward the girls. Although that was amazing and wonderful to grandparents who had reared only boys, Justin was the blue-ribbon boy in a family with two daughters. Only sons with older sisters are lucky. Justin had his natural mother, plus two "little mothers" in Heather and Lesli who loved to play the role. It was a triumph worth crying about for Dorian, gallant woman, "It's a boy!"

In this chapter, I want to take you through the intimately personal events of conception, embryo and fetal development, up to delivery. I want to unfold those events along life's way in a pattern that will link them back to Creation and to Adam—the double-imaged male and female Adam. As we look at the mystery of each creation of a new person, it is not difficult to celebrate in a hymn of thanksgiving. And when it comes to that, Psalm 139 expressed it long ago:

> O Lord, you have searched me
>     and you know me. . . .
> For you created my inmost being;
>     you knit me together in my mother's womb.
> I praise you because I am fearfully
>     and wonderfully made;
> Your works are wonderful,
>     I know that full well.
> My frame was not hidden from you
>     when I was made in the secret place.
> When I was woven together
>     in the depths of the earth,
>     your eyes saw my unformed body. . . .
>                         Psalm 139:13–16

## Win the Creation Sweepstakes!

Have you ever considered the probabilities that you would be born who you are—the exact genetic materials that got together to make you? Consider the basic mathematical factors:

1. Your mother was created with more than a lifetime supply of eggs or ova. They were tapped during her fertile years from pubescence to menopause. They were released at the rate of about one every month.

2. Your father was created with an endless supply of sperm, since they are produced and are not derived from a fixed supply created into the male.

3. At each intimate encounter between your father and your mother, your mother was within about fourteen days of the maturation of one of her eggs, but only a few days

of each month set up the conditions in which the egg would be within reach of the searching live sperm.

4. Your father brought to each encounter about 300,-000,000 live, swimming sperm. These set out on a race, looking for the egg. But in almost every case (some twins and multiple births are an exception), only one sperm is able to bury its head in the egg and be declared the winner. When the winner arrives, the egg sets up an invisible shield which rejects all other sperm.

Now, if your parents were "average" by standards of typical research, they were meeting in this way about three and a half times per week during the decade or so in which their children were born. There is some evidence that if the parents were "born again," or "converted" following the onset of pubescence, they were one full count ahead of the popular rate—coming together nearly five times per week. But take the lower rate and begin multiplying. It will become clear that the possible combinations of sperm and egg are virtually infinite, and that your probabilities of being born "you" are very slim! The ratio of eggs to sperm were 120:3,263,000,000,000! Even if you had to split your chances with two or three brothers and sisters in that ten-year period, you still came off winning one of the wildest random drawings in the history of the world. So congratulate yourself! You are an amazing winner. The extravagance of the Creator is well established. When it comes to guaranteeing diversity, beauty, and fully splendored gifts, God has written it everywhere in the created order.

## Boy or Girl?

When a sperm pierces the egg, conception has been completed. With the egg, the mother always provides an X chromosome. The father may bring either an X or a Y chromosome. An XX combination conceives a baby girl. An XY union starts a boy. But for the first trimester, the baby develops the morphology of a female embryo. That is, the reproductive cells, complete with fallopian tubes and open vaginal tract, all develop in both the XX and XY combination embryos. By the sixth week of development, the XY embryo, which is destined to be a male, places a demand on the mother's supply of androgens—her "male" hormones. Consider the fact that the baby boy must plant himself in the wall of a female uterus and grow there in an estrogen rich environment, yet must become an androgen-dominant person. The mother's supply of androgens is critical to what I want to refer to as the sexual differentiation that occurs in two major transformations.[1] The first is genital, and the second is cortical, having to do with differentiating the brain. Humans are differentiated not only sexually, but in the way the brain is organized.

*Genital Transformation*

Imagine an embryo which is now between the sixth and ninth week of life. It has a distinctly human appearance. By the end of the twelfth week, it will have fingernails. If the baby were lost during these weeks and you examined it carefully, you would likely conclude, "We lost a baby girl." The genital development of a male and a female look almost identical in this early phase. What you could not see, but what a chromosome check would reveal if it were, indeed, a boy, would be the testicles being transformed out of the reproductive cells inside the body where the ovaries would have developed in a girl. The mother's androgens, responding to the XY chromosome command, permit the Y chromosome to produce an alien androgen protein which coats the cells programmed to become ovaries. The coating begins the transformation process which turns them into testicles. Still in the ovarian position in the little embryonic body, the testicles then begin to pump out two androgens. One moves them into the mouth of the fallopian tubes and begins their relocation outside the body. The fallopian tubes serve as the collapsible freeway through which the testicles are transported and relocated outside the body. The same androgen is programmed to absorb the fallopian tubes and to enclose the uterus in the urinary tract. The other androgen produced by the testicles is testosterone, which causes a penis to develop where the clitoris would have developed in an XX chromosome baby.

Consider the transformation. As the testes enter the fallopian tubes, the tubes begin to disappear in the wake of the moving testes. Therefore, no adult male carries any mark that he once had fallopian tubes. But something different happens when the testes come to the uterus. It is somehow enclosed in the urinary tract of the transforming male, and it remains suspended there, visible by microphotography and widely shown in *The Body Human* video series. The testes continue their descent through the vaginal tract. The lips of the vagina seal with the glue of the fetal androgens, and each lip receives one of the arriving testicles. The scrotum is now in place, complete with a perfectly straight scar which runs from the base of the penis to the back, as if a surgeon had opened the scrotum then sewed it up. This elastic skinned bag is a thermostatically controlled environment for the testes, which must remain a constant three degrees below body temperature for sperm to develop and be fertile. The penis is formed where the clitoris forms in the female. It enlarges in response to the testosterone produced by the newly formed testicles. The urinary tract is rerouted, and in addition, the seminal vesicles and prostate system are also formed. All of these changes are made on the "standard female model," given shape by the mother's X chromosome.

## Differentiating the Brain

During the sixteenth week of fetal development, another major modification occurs. If the XY chromosome code is calling for the delivery of a baby boy, the brain must be "changed" from that of a healthy girl to that of a boy. The change agent, again, is the androgen hormone solution.

The standard female brain is organized with a high level of communication between the two hemispheres. These walnut-like halves which spread across the top half of the human head are connected by a communications network called the corpus callosum. When the androgens saturate the male fetal brain, they focus on the left hemisphere and on the corpus callosum. The connection between the hemispheres is greatly simplified, with the effect that the hemispheres will specialize for different functions which tend not to be duplicated in the other hemisphere. In a female, on the other hand, many functions have back-up systems in the opposite hemisphere. For example, since speech production is located almost always in the left hemisphere in both men and women, men tend not to recover speech following a right-side/left-hemisphere stroke nearly so well as do women, who tend to respond more positively to speech therapy.

The boy's brain is primarily altered in the left hemisphere and in the corpus callosum. Besides reducing the communicating capacity of the corpus callosum, the left hemisphere is saturated by androgens, which give it a slight setback. As with the reproductive cells, the left hemisphere is coated by androgens and its function is specialized. This modification procedure between the sixteenth and twenty-sixth week seems to account for the rather larger number of boys, as compared to girls, who become candidates for the speech pathologist's attention when they arrive at school. In some communities these boys outnumber girls by as much as nine to one.

The findings about this differentiation of the brain are so new we may consider that we are standing on the threshold of an entirely new set of insights about male and female differences. But the early reports seem to underscore our insights here pointing to the absolute interdependence of male and female and of their complementarity. The "splitting of the Adam" appears to occur at every Creation of a new human baby.

Diane McGuinness of Stanford University supervises research on sex differences. She stands at the front of a long line of researchers, mostly women, who appeal for differentiated care for boys as compared to girls. In her significant report, "How Schools Discriminate Against Boys," she points out how mothers, teachers, and physicians often conspire against normal testosterone-driven activity levels in boys and put them on Ritalin, a drug which acts to tranquilize normal boys to make them acceptable to the demands of a crowded classroom. That room, in most cases, is controlled to the activity level demands of a woman teacher.

While an occasional child no doubt needs help with "hyperactivity," it is McGuinness' contention that the drug has become a quick fix for many boys who are well within the normal range of activity.[2]

McGuinness reports that about 10 percent of schoolchildren are on prescription Ritalin to "reduce their disruptive behavior to docility." She indicates that studies show that "once diagnosed as hyperactive, they are likely to develop social and psychiatric disorders such as depression and to fail in school far more often than normal children with the same IQ scores and ability." She holds that once a child is labeled a "deviant, the distress caused by the stigma is difficult to erase."

In the Stanford studies of children—with their focus on identifying differences between boys and girls—an experimental laboratory was set up in which children had opportunities to work at a number of different tasks, according to their choice. The researchers observed children for twenty minutes per child. Several girls, but only one boy, maintained constant attention for a twenty-minute period. The others had scores for only part of the block of time. The average time a girl worked at one task was 12.5 minutes; the average boy worked 6.5 minutes per task. Boys interrupted what they were doing almost twice as often as girls. Girls finished nearly everything they started; boys finished only half of their starts. For the boys, a new category had to be added: watching others. They spent 4.5 minutes "watching." The boys also tackled twice as many three-dimensional tasks as girls attempted. One third of the boys took toys apart; none of the girls did. All in all, the differences suggested some intrinsic differences:

*Vocalization.* Girls monitored their entire activity and time with speech, almost continuously, offered advice and information, and asked for help. It was recorded that "Boys made more noises, uttered commands and expletives, and used more abrupt phrases such as 'Look at me.' " Although boys and girls produced the same amount of vocalization, 40 percent of the boys' noisemaking was not syntactical speech.

*Three-dimensional vision.* Boys were twice as fast in constructing three-dimensional objects from building blocks as were girls. Much of the time boys were "watching," they appeared to be doing three-dimensional experiments. They stood with arms akimbo and, by moving their bodies, appeared to be watching the "movement" of objects in their visual field. Other researchers have linked such three-dimensional fascination with later excellence in abstract mathematics such as geometry. "Sex differences are found only in tests of higher mathematics," McGuinness reports; there are "no sex differences in tests of arithmetic."

*Activity.* "Boys cannot sit still," McGuinness observes. They are easily distracted. They have to test the property of objects, even take them apart. Such behavior "interferes with the concentration they need to learn to read and write. . . . Yet much of this behavior is precisely that which leads to excellence in mechanics, mathematics, and the physical sciences," McGuinness says.

*Optic system.* Other studies cited by McGuinness show that females adapt more quickly to night vision than do males, but that females "continue to see the afterimage of a spot of light longer than males." The opposite is true in daylight. Women tend to have more problems meeting traffic in night driving, but men see afterimages of high contrast in full daylight. They are more sensitive to optical afterimages related to welding, for example. But men are better able to follow a moving target in daylight. And men consistently choose lower light levels for working than do women.

*Musculature.* Rough-and-tumble play is almost exclusively a male activity. Roughly 40 percent of the male body tissue at maturity will be muscle, while only about 23 percent of the female body will be in the musculature. The woman's investment in fatty tissue is critical, since the estrogens that support her fertility will be stored and utilized from the fatty tissue. In terms of muscle expertise, then, males tend to excel in gross motor skill and eye-muscle coordination. Females, however, tend to excel in finer motor/muscle skills and coordination.

*Immune system.* Birth trauma or other irregularities during embryo and fetal development are often associated with allergy problems in early life, especially with boys. All of this is rooted in the basic immunity system which seems especially sensitive in males, no doubt because of the sexual-differentiation tasks of the male fetus. Left-handedness, while easily traced in most families to heredity factors, also seems to be more often associated with birth or fetal trauma than with normal development and delivery.

*Sexual attraction.* There is mounting evidence that the male attraction to the female is also programmed during the sexual differentiation of the brain.[3] One study points to the period in which the male brain is being transformed from the basically female brain as a critical time for the mother's male hormones, the androgens, to initiate the work. It is speculated that any sort of interruption of the mother's androgens, as sometimes occurs in times of severe stress or when the mother has developed a tumor of the ovary, may "deprive" the male fetus of androgens, thus leaving a partially differentiated brain. An ovarian tumor, for example, tends to produce its own source of estrogens, thus saturating the fetus with female hormones that interfere with the delicate brain transformation. Since sexual arousal is produced in both males and females by the secretion of a chemical deep in the brain—which almost instantly is carried to the genitals where the flow of blood is restricted, enlarging the organs—the "brain source" for sexual arousal is clear. While sexual arousal is no doubt also related to environmental factors such as early experience and family expectation and encouragement, there is now little doubt that a potential danger exists that same-sex preference may be rooted in a malformation during the sixteenth to the twenty-sixth weeks of a pregnancy. No similar danger exists for a girl, since the mother's supply of estrogens is not in danger of being displaced by androgens, and since "normal development" of any fetus proceeds along the female development pattern.

### The Dominican "Laboratory"

In a remote section of the Dominican Republic, a physician on holiday in 1950 discovered first one, then a group that now numbers thirty-eight mutant-defect males who began life with complete female external genitalia. The group, spanning four generations and twenty-three interrelated families, was rediscovered in 1972.[4] They have been systematically studied by Dr. Julianne Imperato-McGinley and other colleagues of hers at the division of endocrinology in the school of medicine at Cornell University in New York.

Of the twenty-five surviving postpubertal "boys," nineteen have been studied carefully, using local dialect interviews to assess the developmental histories. All were reared as girls. Their bodies, while formed with apparent normal levels of their mothers' androgens, did not develop full male genitalia because a mutant genetic defect prevented their bodies from being able to process testosterone or dihydrotestosterone. The latter hormone is the one which seems to be responsible for giving the final shape to the external genitalia. Therefore, the boys were born with an apparent female system, but deep inside, the female parts had already been absorbed and the testicles were waiting to descend. The brain development is assumed to have been normal male transformation. This is suggested by the fact that of the nineteen boys who were reared unambiguously as girls, seventeen assumed male "sexual identity" when, at pubescence, the testicles descended, the scrotum formed, and the penis developed. By "sexual identity" the researchers meant that the boys saw themselves as males, felt like males. Of the group, sixteen immediately assumed a male "sex role," by which the researchers meant they moved socially so as to send off appropriate signals as males.

The significance of the Dominican males to our understanding of sexual differentiation is still being weighed. The Cornell group suggests that the mutant gene may have performed an experiment for us which our own research ethics would never permit. They are impressed with the fact that in an isolated part of a primitive culture we have been allowed to see that how a child is reared may not be able to scramble the biological identity written in the brain. These boys—whose only bathing option was the public bath in the river, and whose external sexual identification was widely known—stemmed the tide of public ridicule, name calling, and labeling. All but one of them followed local male practice and took up common-law marriages, with only a one-year delay in taking up male sexual practice when compared with normal males in their communities. The one exception lives "as a woman" but is sexually active as a male, indicating clear male sexual identity, but choosing to retain the female sex role.

## The Double-Adam

In Creation, Adam was split to form both the female and the male. But in every re-creation moment, embryo development is programmed to form either an XX girl or an XY boy. And, in either case, the mother's delicate balance of androgens and estrogens controls the precise sex form of the developing baby.

The mother's hormonal balance can be disturbed, however, and with a reproductive system saturated with estrogens, the baby boy may be born with confused genitals and brain, or with genitals which appear to be entirely female. And if the mother is treated with the male androgens during her pregnancy with an XX girl, the baby may be born with what appear to be male genitals, and the brain may be likewise differentiated by the saturation with androgens at a critical moment.

Where normal development occurs, it is clear that Creation still forms both male and female out of the same "stuff." "Adam" is our first name and our first form. And the differentiation is so profound that each side of Adam is left with a yearning for the other. The "magnet" of Eden draws them back to the one-flesh attachment by which Adam is made complete: male and female.

We stand on tiptoe, then, confessing that the witnesses agree: We are fearfully and wonderfully made. Elizabeth Barrett Browning once addressed that reverence, which may overwhelm us in the presence of "ordinary" routine miracles:

> Earth's crammed with heaven,
> And every common bush afire with God;

But only he who sees take off his shoes;
The rest sit round it and pluck blackberries.[5]

## QUESTIONS PEOPLE ASK

*Q: This is all a little shocking. I went through nurses training, and I never went over this version of embryo and fetal development. What is going on?*
A: It isn't at all clear why embryology has been taught as it has been in the past. Here are the alternate ways sexual development used to be taught (you may recognize your instruction among them):

1. Virtually ignore sexual development in the first six to ten weeks of life. It was typical to make a sweeping comment that during these weeks the embryo was "undifferentiated" or "neutral." Some came close to the truth with the humorous paradox: "The neutral sex is female."

2. Gloss over sexual differentiation with technical jargon, which the professors themselves may have not clearly understood: "The male is homogametic while the female is heterogametic."

3. Stress that the differentiating hormone is androgen; yet, typically, there was no reporting or hypothesizing what might happen if the androgen were absent and what form the body would continue to develop, or why. M. J. Sherfey, whose work I first found cited in a recent handbook on psychiatry, reports:

> The innate femaleness of mammalian embryos was firmly established between 1957–58 (with, of course, over fifteen years of prior research); but the biologists recorded the fact with little comment. Although some of us might question the motivation behind their lack of interest in this startling discovery which overturns centuries of mythology and years of scientific theory, it could be expected since the biologists had long considered the "bisexuality" of the "undifferentiated" phase to be of no prime importance.[6]

All of us stand to benefit from each new breakthrough in understanding the Creation through understanding human growth and development. I have sometimes said that "our theology is often little better than our biology." It would appear ironic, if not important, that the new "truth in embryology" should surface at about the same moment that courageous women entered the research laboratories. Dr. Mary Jane Sherfey, M. D., stops appropriately short of making any accusations about the past.

*Q: Three and a half times per week seems pretty high for the marital intimacy you use in computing "probabilities" on conception. Where do these statistics come from?*

A: Research based on "volunteer" samples is vulnerable to bragging, and it is also likely to attract people who are willing, even eager, to talk about intimate matters. The original Alfred Kinsey work, while now more than thirty years old, avoided the volunteer problems and even weeded out persons during interviews if they seemed eager to tell their story. The "3.5" is a Kinsey mean or average. Measured in "male output," Kinsey found the frequency to run from .5 to 21 times per week in "range."[7]

Some of the more recent studies suggest that "religious women" are both more exclusive (one man in a lifetime) and more sexually active.[8] This matches recent negative trends in France and lends credence to the idea that pornography and the sexual revolution may actually reduce the frequency of sexual intimacy. The so-called sex magazines may turn out to be really anti-sex. In a follow-up interview after *Redbook* magazine had identified "religious women as better lovers," the editors reported the judgment of a Jesuit priest from Loyola University. When he was asked what was wrong with all of these religious women who were so sexually active, he replied, "It seems to me you are asking the wrong question. You should be asking what is wrong with all of the other women."

*Q: You quote Diane McGuinness as charging that mothers and teachers and physicians conspire to prescribe Ritalin when children are only normal, not hyperactive. Don't some children need medication for hyperactivity?*

A: No doubt some children do need temporary medication to help them cope with stress that shows itself in restlessness and hyperactivity. But "hyperactivity" is an ambiguous term, and physicians who specialize in child treatment will tend not to misuse Ritalin. No doubt Dr. McGuinness is reporting on long-term studies of children who should not have been given Ritalin. That drug is evidently a highly specific one, with very positive effects for children who are diagnosed as suffering from "attention deficit disorder." This problem shows up in children who seem unable to focus on what is happening around them, largely because brain images are not making sense to them. It is related to the more common letter reversals in which children cannot discriminate between $d$ and $b$ and are often diagnosed as dyslectics.

You may find that some university near you maintains, as the University of Kentucky does near me, a Hyperkinetic Clinic operated as a family-practice arm of its medical school. Before settling for long-term medication for a child, it is important to have consultative medical advice. A physician may even suggest a chromosome check for a boy. Should the rare implantation of a sperm carrying a double YY code show up, the combined XYY boy is likely to have a genetically based hyperactivity. Physicians are obligated both legally and ethically to advise the family in such a case and to help them seek both medical and social assistance in dealing with the rather enormous energy and activity levels of this rare syndrome. Where emotional factors or dietary triggers such as food coloring, additives, bleaches, and the like are identified as contributing to high activity levels, it is urgent that non-chemical solutions be found and the child be taken off Ritalin or other tranquilizing drugs as soon as possible.

*Q: Could you say more about "anomalous dominance," or the cross-wiring of the brain in relation to eyes and hands?*

A: I can say more, of course, and I will. Let me first tell you that I am searching for more published research on this amazing discovery. All of the new findings are rooted in the Nobel Prizewinning work of Roger Sperry at Cal Tech. He introduced surgery to save the lives of epileptic victims whose "electrical storms of the brain" were reducing them to serious seizures every few minutes—a life-threatening condition. These wonderful people survived the separation of the two hemispheres. The corpus callosum was severed—the neurological "telegraph lines" connecting the two halves of the brain. By carefully studying their abilities after the surgery, we now have a picture of what goes on in the hemispheres. Carl Sagan has popularized the work of Sperry in his book, *The Dragons of Eden*.[9]

Here are some of my first-hand observations:

1. In any room full of persons who check eye dominance, there are as many combinations of "strength of dominance" as there are people in the room. We are uniquely individual in brain organization. Creation is everywhere characterized by diversity, even within categories! To do a simple check, simply hold up your thumb at arm's length and—with both eyes open—line it up with a vertical line across the room. Move it back and forth until you are satisfied that it is in the best position. Almost all of us get a double image, but you can find the "best" line-up. Now close your left eye. If your thumb is crisply on the target, you are right-eye dominant. If your thumb appears to jump sideways, start over and close the right eye to check for left-eye dominance. There are many people for whom neither eye remains exactly on target. When you try to count the variations in the room, you will conclude that each person is unique. If the thumb jumps sideways, for example, it does not jump the same distance for all, even though the majority will be distinctly on target with right eyes. *Anomalous dominance* refers to any combination in which the dominant eye differs from the hand of preference. People who shoot a gun, and have to cross over the barrel to "sight with" the eye opposite to the trigger hand, know that they are cross dominant.

2. Many persons with anomalous dominance are nicely and effectively coordinated. This seems always to be true, in my experience, with "mirror twins." And they tend strongly to be also mirrored in that one will be left-handed and the other right-handed. Since there is evidence that many of us are the survivor in a twin conception in which one of the twins did not survive long after conception, the

nicely coordinated anomalous-dominant people may, in some cases, be such survivors.

3. Some persons with anomalous dominance were obviously changed to right-handed behavior when they started school, or earlier, by anxious parents. Not all of these people experience any difficulty, although some tell me they feel "high-strung," and one postal clerk who, at age fifty, was undergoing a piecework evaluation reported that throwing first class mail at mail slots was a problem. He said that he consistently mis-threw letters by about one-quarter inch, missing the slot to one side. I urged him to try that long-dormant left hand. The left hand in most of us is capable of greater precision, anyway. And in the Old Testament there were seven hundred soldiers who "could sling a stone at a hair and not miss." The text makes it explicit: they were all left-handed and from the same tribe (see Judges 20:16). Precision, dexterity, and artistic ability are more often associated with left-handedness than with the right.[10] The list of top artists is studded with left-handed men: Michelangelo, daVinci, Picasso, to name a few. And left-handed male surgeons are renowned for their precision.

4. Many times the anomalous dominance is present in males who have experienced much frustration with school. Here are two cases with which I am presently working:

(a) T has a degree in engineering. He is left-handed but right-eye dominant. "I would just like to take notes for one semester with somebody else's brain," he told me. He reports that even the most ordinary words escape him while he is trying to take notes. And when he tries to organize a written report or a research paper, he freezes up. On one occasion I talked him through some of the basic exercises in G. L. Rico's *Writing the Natural Way*.[11] He plotted the contents of his research on one of the global planning grids. Result: a paper designed by the right hemisphere which connected with his "languaging" hand.

(b) J has now graduated from college, but I followed him through semesters at two undergraduate schools. He is the most profoundly cross-brained man I have seen. One evening late at my house, he excused himself from a conversation between his fiancée, himself, and me. He went to my front porch and howled for a couple of minutes. The sound was almost like the coyote cry with which I grew up in western Kansas! I asked his fiancée, "Does he often do that?" She replied, "Whenever he is under stress he often does it, and it seems to help." On dozens of occasions when J walks in on me with a good deal of excitement, he bursts into highly verbal, seemingly coherent speech. But I am consistently unable to "track" with him. My standard interruption is, "Can you say that another way? I'm not following what you are saying." And with a second version, I am almost always with him. Now the most striking thing about J's school performance is that almost without exception he is summoned for a conference following any written report or research paper. The professors at both colleges boldly accused J of turning in material he had not himself written. He is so effectively wired into written language that people who have known him mainly through oral communication conclude that he has stolen the written work. J is now enrolled at a great university as a non-matriculated student in the graduate school. He is trying to rescue a poor transcript by proving that he can handle the tough standards of graduate study. In J's case, as with so many anomalous dominant males, he is aware that he has competences which he cannot successfully demonstrate on standard left-brained school performance tests.

In a 1982 paper published in the *Proceedings of the National Academy of Sciences,* Geschwind and Behan of Glasgow University reported some of the effects of anomalous dominance.[12] They studied more than 2,000 people—analyzing how they write, throw a ball, and unscrew a bottle cap and other behavior—to establish brain- and hand-dominance. Eventually, they found 500 who were clearly left-handed and 900 who were distinctly right-handed. "Around 10 percent of the left-handers reported some form of developmental problems like dyslexia or stuttering," Geschwind says, "while in right-handers only 1 percent did." A *Newsweek* summary of the report continues: Eleven percent of the left-handers had immunity diseases such as allergies, compared to four percent of right handers. But relatives of left-handers with immunity problems were also more likely to be afflicted with them, suggesting a genetic basis which also correlates with handedness. The culprit is believed to be the hormone testosterone, "the hormone that produces the biggest differences between the sexes." Males are saturated with testosterone from early fetal development, and left-handedness shows up in males at a 10 percent rate compared to 6 percent rate in females. Besides differentiating the brain, even slowing the growth of the left hemisphere in the male, it now appears that testosterone may be reducing the size of the thymus gland in these left-handed, immunity troubled males. It is the thymus gland which enables the body to distinguish its own tissues from transplants. Without these recognizer cells, the body attacks its own tissues. This characteristic causes speculation that these people may also be more resistant to cancers and infections. The Glasgow scholars report: "Something is increasing the rate of all these conditions—left-handedness, learning disabilities and autoimmune disease." They are at a loss to account for such a trend by using conventional evolutionary hypotheses regarding natural selection. The most Geschwind can say is that it "is nature's way of increasing diversity of brains." They—and we—are aware that unusual creativity arises at a very high rate from these irregularly formed neurological brains.

There is little doubt but that all of us enhance our use of the brain when we use both eyes and both hands. It may be an important experiment for the anomalous-dominant brain to try the following:

*Piano lessons.* Any keyboard instrument which requires the use of both hands will activate both hemispheres, and any form of music production or listening engages the affective/feeling hemisphere from which ecstasy and worship arise. Most musical instruments require the use of both hands in manipulating keys or strings. It is important to encourage "playing by ear" or simply improvising, creating the image of sounds out of one's own imagination—a distinctly right-hemisphere activity. Mechanical playing may be entirely left-hemisphere dominant.

*Storytelling/listening.* This type of activity engages the right hemisphere. Jesus always used parables because he came to change beliefs and commitments. Today's most effective preachers are gifted storytellers.

*Typing and word-processing.* Put your child onto a computer-based operation which requires the use of both hands on a keyboard. You may be surprised what happens when both hemispheres are accessed in this amazing way. It is likely that video games are awakening right-hemisphere competence, and it is not surprising that their appeal is chiefly to males, since the male brain is amazingly specialized to eye-hand coordination.

Since we stand on a frontier in understanding brain organization, I would urge parents or anomalous-dominant men themselves to contact their nearest university. Try to reach someone in "neurosurgery" or "neuropsychology." Ask for recent articles which might help you to understand yourself or your child. We will no doubt step across the threshold within the next five years. In the meantime, remember that teachers and other professionals are often lagging at least one generation of knowledge behind the great research breakthroughs. Share with those who work with your child anything you may turn up at the university.

*Q: Why is it that so many males experience some sexual ambiguity as they enter adulthood? At our college there are several of us who are not really sure what attracts us sexually.*

A: There are three votes cast in every election of so-called sexual identity: (1) biology, consisting of the genital and brain resources; (2) family and environment, and their encouragement of "sex role"; and (3) you and your own choice about sexual identity—how you choose to feel about yourself and to project your sexual identity in the community. For most of us, all of the votes agree and the male feels and projects like a male. For some, bickering between father and mother may have sent some hidden messages to the effect that "it may not be such a good idea to be a male." The recent book *The Peter Pan Syndrome* is an excellent resource to look at how both the father and the mother may give off signals to a boy that he may never want to become a man.[13] Our playboy culture is heavily populated with Peter Pan types who refuse to grow up and want to avoid the responsibilities of the adult male. Ultimately, all research agrees, the veto power over the first two factors resides in the third. Every person chooses both who to "be" and what image to project to the community.

The Masters and Johnson clinic in St. Louis reports transformation of sexual orientation by "Type 6 Kinsey Males" (homosexually oriented) who chose to veto all other factors. Alfred Kinsey's study of 12,000 males gave us the first tangible clue that male sexual orientation is not a simple matter of "heterosexual" versus "homosexual."[14] In tabulating his findings of the pattern in male imagination and experience, Kinsey found it necessary to plot seven categories of male orientation. At each end were the totally heterosexual and the totally homosexual categories, but the four between were mixed. They included some combinations of each kind of imagination and of experience.

Kinsey also found that 37 percent of the males in the study had experienced at least one mutual orgasmic experience with another male. No similar findings emerged for females. And since the male hydraulic system brings on a full sexual appetite soon after sexual maturity, the male is more prone to take up active social sexual experience or to develop a substantial pattern of masturbation than is the female. Kinsey's males showed no visible change in frequency of ejaculation at marriage, for example, and continued the 3.5-per-week pattern as a mean. Recent studies which set out to correct Kinsey's research with women have focused on masturbation, only to show that the mean frequency for women who volunteer their data (Kinsey did not work with a volunteer sample, with its tendencies toward exhibitionism) find that among women who do masturbate—and not all do—the frequency stands at a mean of twenty-four times per year.

Given the assurance that brain differentiation is powerful enough to override public labeling, as in the case of the Dominican sample, it should not be surprising if we were to find that not all male brains differentiate to the "Type 0 Kinsey Male" category. The Dorner study from Germany suggests that lowered androgen levels between the sixteenth and twenty-sixth weeks of fetal development may leave the brain in a male fetus virtually undifferentiated from its female standard form.[15] In such a case, sexual arousal, which begins with brain chemistry and response to imagination or visual/tactile stimulation, would be programmed to homosexual preference. What is clear is that males fall along this spectrum in such a way that we should not be surprised to find perhaps up to 37 percent of males experiencing some ambiguity.

In my experience, I encourage a young male to dispense with labels all together and to decide what kinds of feelings he prefers to cultivate. I regret that a political issue has been made which puts forward a label with which the young have to deal during the years when sexual orientation may be ambiguous. But if Masters and Johnson are able to see transformation of established adult "Type 6" males, we should not be reluctant to surround any young male among us with all the affirmation he needs to both own and possess his full identity and role as a male.[16]

# 6

# Birth Bonding: Bring on the "Double Adam"

△

With a little practice, most of us show improved abilities. My wife and I are better "parents" to our grandchildren than we were to our two sons. And, I must say, they and their wives are better parents than we were at their own stage of experience.

With more than fifty years clocked in the human race, some of it sharply tuned to matters of human development, I have done a bit of coaching when so-called new discoveries popped up. So, less than sixty days before the birth of Number Six grandchild, I breathlessly recited "birth bonding" news to Mike and Dorian. I had phoned the University of Kentucky medical center library in hopes of renting a film on birth bonding. They wanted, they said, to sell it to me "cheaply." It turns out they had found a better one—a film-strip, actually. "Then, that's what I want to rent," I said, never afraid of buying the latest model of most things.

Robbie and I spent the night at Mike's place. Dorian was in labor, and we were to be the sleep-through baby-sitters for Heather and Lesli. At about five in the morning, we got the signal that Dorian was ready to go. I was scheduled to fly out of Lexington for Lycoming College in Pennsylvania, where I was lecturing at a congress on evangelism for the Northeastern Jurisdiction of the United Methodist

108

Church. Mike and Dorian dropped me at Bluegrass Field and proceeded to Central Baptist Hospital.

When I completed my first address just before noon, the moderator came to the podium and announced, "You will be glad to know that Dr. Joy has just become the grandfather of his sixth grandchild, a boy."

I was ecstatic, of course, for reasons I explained in the last chapter. Naturally, I phoned the hospital to inquire about name, weight, and the health of both mother and baby. Everyone was fine, I was told, but neither name nor weight were available. I waited for a while and phoned again after lunch—still no news. At the nurses' station, I evoked this response: "We would like to know those things, too. We haven't had a chance even to see the baby. Its parents won't let us have it to clean it up, to weigh it, or to get its name recorded. They've been in there for more than three hours."

When Mike and Dorian had asked their physician, Dr. Alan David, about having "birth bonding time" of up to two hours, he hesitated, since he had never before made arrangements for that much exclusive time with the baby. But he agreed to clear the procedure with hospital staff. The only thing that could interfere, he explained, would be some unforeseen complication with the delivery. Five of our six grandchildren have been delivered by physicians from the University of Kentucky's family practice unit. Only Jami Maree—born, as her brother Jason used to say at three, "in Minneapolisota"—missed the UK doctors.

I was eager to arrive back in Lexington on the third day of Justin's introduction to this planet. He was in my arms within a minute of my arrival. I took him gingerly, with feelings that matched the first holding of my own sons. And, with the same clumsiness, I placed his head on my left arm and tried to snuggle him around my front. It felt as if his head were going to fall off the fat of my lower arm, and surely enough, it did! But not because of my clumsiness. The kid had fixed his eyes on Mike as his daddy had walked past me to the front door. The little newborn was actually using the new musculature of his neck to twist and pitch his eyes around a corner to see the man to whom he was birth-bonded.

We were to see other effects of the birth-bonding time. This was to be the most peaceable baby we had ever been around. His whimpering became articulated almost immediately, different signals indicating particular needs he had. And there was no wailing in the night, no anxiety, but only a deep attachment to both mother and father which transferred easily to other humans. It was an amazingly comfortable feeling to be around him.

## The Magic Moments

We have been aware for a long time of the critical first minutes after birth during which animal mothers "own" their young. Any farmer who has presided over the arrival of lambs or calves, or any family that has witnessed the birth of a litter of pups or kittens knows that the mother's first attention is almost a smothering approach. There is smelling and licking, accompanied by vocalizations unique to the after-birth minutes.

On a cold February night long ago, I was helping my dad with ewes who chose the night of a Kansas blizzard to deliver. Each of us was fully occupied with separate delivering ewes. I had just reported a pair of healthy twins. Dad was having trouble. Finally, he had the lamb, but it was dead; he tried but could not get it breathing. "Give me one of those twins," he said. I carried one to him. Then I watched him gather up the placenta which he had just drawn from the ewe whose lamb was dead. He smeared the alien twin with the placenta. Thoroughly. Then he stood the wobbly animal near the nose of the ewe whose lamb was stillborn. I was amazed. The odor had worked magic and deception on her; she now "owned" the lamb and it began to nurse.

What we knew in animal husbandry was finally studied "scientifically" by Konrad Lorenz fifty years ago. He found that newly hatched chickens will adopt any moving object as "Mother" in a critical period of time during which the depth and persistence of attachment seems to be greatest.

With humans, however, science took us in another direction. "Safe, painless childbirth" became the marvelous gift of the fifties. By all of this, the medical community intended to present a package in which (a) the mother was immobilized by drugs, often injected in the spinal column; (b) the mother was reduced to an extended period of several hours of semiconscious "shadowland," during which time she would have no memory of delivery or of her child; and (c) the doctors would do everything, including dragging the baby down the birth canal with forceps. It is not surprising that this medical wonder preceded by just about twenty years violence and turbulence of a generation of our young who were labeled "The Alienated."

Finally, some scientists have begun to ask whether there may be a critical period with newborn humans during which attachment to the mother and the father may be critical. While many physicians and most hospitals continue to resist birth-bonding time, many are open to parents who request an opportunity to do what all parents instinctually want to do—have immediate time with their young. The best research findings about birth bonding point to these facts:[1]

*Critical time.* There is a period of heightened sensitivity to attachment. It seems to last for up to three hours following delivery. Sensitivity to parents or any stimulus tends to wane following that time.

*Vision.* The newborn has a heightened visual acuity, with focusing capacity that matches adult vision, in which a "zoom lens" ability is able to focus on any object near or far. However, within a few hours after birth, the baby's vision will tend to become fixed at a focal length of about ten inches (the distance between breast and mother's face), with all else blurred out of focus. The visual acuity equips the newborn with search ability to locate the object to which to bond. In these first few hours the baby's vision and muscle control is so heightened that it will mimic parental "faces," such as sticking out the tongue. But these responses tend to fade and do not reappear for several weeks.

*Hearing.* The human mother tends to vocalize at the sight of her newborn, using sounds she does not normally use. These tend to be "helium-like," high-pitched speech to which the newborn is especially responsive. The newborn quickly turns to follow sound as well as sight, with sensitivities and abilities which will recede after the first few hours.

*Touch.* Skin-to-skin contact, literally galvanic connections, appear to have important effects on attachment. Fathers are often advised to remove shirts so that both the warmth of the body and the magic of skin contact can communicate "ownership" and affection to the infant. The effects on parents of this naked contact are predictably powerful. We have only begun to discover the powerful effects of touch on enhancing body chemistry and the tendency to thrive, in premature babies and in the disease-ridden elderly, for example. We may register this as a first axiom: You will become attached to whatever you touch!

*Kiss.* Mouth-to-mouth contact, universal in animals, starts up the digestive system by providing the benign bacterial base for healthy digestion of food. The infant must pick up this bacteria from some human source, and humans are programmed to provide the bacteria by the instinct to nuzzle and kiss the baby.

So, what would a mother and a father normally be doing for two and a half hours after the delivery of their baby? Well, no one has to write the script for them. They are programmed by the Creator to do the right things, if they are only given the opportunity. What is more, these tend to be the most spiritually sensitive hours in the lives of the young adults. However much they may be inclined to think of the baby as "something we have made together," in those first hours they will be quite aware that "this is a miracle, and we have been joined by a special gift from heaven."

We weep—those of us who were ripped from our unconscious mothers and were thrust into antiseptic steel cribs in hermetically sealed nurseries with a half-dozen other screaming babies who, like ourselves, were ripped from their comatose mothers. We weep at the deficit of attachment we have assumed was normal. We weep at the adversary positions we took against our parents without provocation. And those of us whose children were whisked away by a prophylactic nursing staff, to be returned to us often begrudgingly, from four to six hours later, may be inclined to mount an insurrection against the medical pro-

fession and the hospitals. Robbie was reprimanded for un-
wrapping the blanket to get her first glimpse of our Michael.
At prestigious Florence Nightingale, the children's wing
of the famous Baylor Hospital in Dallas, he had been taken
away and detained for four hours, although there were no
medical complications. The fastidious nurse scolded Robbie
for wanting to count toes and examine the whole body of
her no-longer "newborn" son who had been kept from her
for the entire bonding period. But we were, all of us, part
of a generation which picked up the tab on necessary, if
inhumane, medical experimentation which, thankfully, is
beginning now to return to us the opportunities for which
humans were created.

*Presenting Gifts*

The critical bonding period that extends up to about three
hours following birth might be regarded as the time during
which parents and infants "present gifts" to each other.
By this analogy, the interference of medical policy or per-
sonnel with the bonding process might be likened to *How
the Grinch Stole Christmas.*[2] The gifts consist simply of
"ourselves." Here, as in all of life's intimacies, the best experiences are free; they arise out of the magnificence of the
basic human endowment. The Creator has made the resources standard equipment on all models. For this reason,
rich and poor, the homely and the beautiful, absolutely all
of us, are equally endowed to experience all of life's best
moments. Here are some of the gifts we bring:
  *Odor.* The unique aroma of the lanolin-laced lining of
the placenta covers the newborn with a gentle skin treatment which has a unique odor. This odor appears to trigger
"encompassing" gesturing in the mother, sometimes almost
involuntarily—enhancing the desire to hold, to cradle, and
to embrace her baby. This odor has been observed to trigger
similar responses in other women present at the delivery.
When I asked John LeMasters, one of my students, whether
he noticed a particular odor at the birth of his newborn
Jessica, he was ecstatic. "You know how Johnson's Baby
Powder smells?" he asked. "It was something like that, only

better!" And parents, in the universal human tradition, bring their own particular odors to present to the child—odors which will trigger the "at home" sensation for a lifetime. Wise baby-sitters always know which closet to raid to don a piece of Mother's or Father's clothing when they try to comfort a baby who is restless in the absence of the parents. There is enough of a parent's unique odor in a housecoat or other unlaundered garment to remind the infant of the security of being in a safe environment. The first responses of humans tend to place more weight on nonverbal sense messages; and odor is such a powerful resource. Try to recall some of the odors of your early life. Sometimes I am overwhelmed by the smell of homemade eggnog, because my mother, on the physician's suggestion, tried to offset some of my early weakness by enhancing my diet with the raw eggs she could smuggle to me in my eggnog. She made it into a special party. Those memories go back into about my third year, and the odor of eggnog (not the factory kind), with its generous nutmeg seasoning, awakens a pleasant nostalgia in me.

*Voice.* Human mothers tend to elevate their voices and to speak directly to their infants on sight of them. Ewes, too, produce vocalizations at the sight and smell of their own newly born lambs that are never produced at any other time in the life cycle. Recent birth-bonding studies indicate that human mothers also seem programmed to speak to the newborn in a high-pitched voice, to which the infant seems unusually attentive, perhaps because the mother's voice moves into a tonal frequency to which the infant is "pre-tuned."

*Eyes.* Visual bonding is easily identified in all phases of human experience. Watch a father-absent child, for example, and you are likely to see extended stares sent in the direction of a person the child is unconsciously longing for as a father substitute. Potential lovers tend to find that their almost involuntary fixation with looking at the newly discovered person is feeding their addiction to the friendship or to the fantasy. Newborns whose mothers do not stare at their infants tend not to thrive, a clue we picked up directly from monkey studies in which the mortality pattern was virtually inevitable if either the infant or the mother did not spend extended time gazing at the other. We now know that newborn humans have amazingly sophisticated visual acuity. Contrary to the popular folklore, they are able to focus clearly, to follow moving objects with their eyes, even turning their heads to follow. And they can focalize with the full adult capability of the "zoom lens" which puts everything in focus regardless of distance. Within a few hours, however, the infant vision blurs except at the fixed focal length of ten to twelve inches—limiting visual bonding to the face of the feeding parent in the major human contact time. The zoom capacity will return after several weeks.

*Warmth.* The parents' bodies joined to the infant provide a source of stabilization of body temperature during the first few hours of life. The newborn has never had to produce its own body heat alone. Hospital equipment, usually heat lamps, assist with the temperature control, but the attachment to the parents is enhanced by the sense of magnetic warmth which they represent in the first embraces.

*Touch.* Skin-to-skin contact is critical to humans throughout life. Hugging is a ritual form of touch, but so also are the shaking of hands, the patting of the shoulder, the kiss, and much of parent-child teasing. The mother's nude body is an ideal bonding surface for the nude infant, and the first hours should bring them together for sealing the "peaceable kingdom" relationship. Fathers are often coached by the physician to remove their shirts down to the skin, since the galvanic contact is as equally effective between infant and father as with the mother.

Here, again, it is clear that the Creator equips humans with the "best things in life," and "free," too. A healthy woman and a healthy man are fully equipped and programmed to produce a child and to attach themselves to the child and the child to them. Like the "rain which falls on the just and the unjust" and the sun which shines on the good and the evil, so also God's prevenient grace is everywhere evident as a free gift to all. And in the sense seen by John Wesley so long ago, that prevenient grace is always a witness to God's own character. All of life's basic intimacies are characterized by this "witness" content. The image of God laid down in our sexual identity, male and female, becomes, indeed "the first curriculum."

## The Peaceable Kingdom

"You gave me some insight into my parent's family today in this address," a minister nearing retirement said to me. "There were eight children. I was the sixth. We were all born at home. I have wondered why all of us remained both close to our parents and faithful to the parents' beliefs and values. Now, I think I can understand our closeness and also I can see why so many of today's children are alienated from their parents and from traditional values. I am told that when I was born, my mother delivered in the 'attached parsonage' and that the congregation was singing 'Love Lifted Me' through the wall that separated the bedroom from the sanctuary where a revival service was in progress."

Such "primitive birthing practices" seem appalling to our antiseptic ears. And most of us hope that modern birthing space and arrangements become an option at all hospitals with maternity services. But the fact is, parent-child bonding is not limited to the first three hours of life. The same principles and the same resources are valid throughout life.

Adoptive parents wisely invest time in skin contact, face-to-face communication, and in frequent stroking of the child's sense of selfhood. How many hugs does it take to get the adult chemistry up to the standards of simple health maintenance? Some wholistic health authorities think at least half a dozen per day are minimal needs.

Dale had adopted Carl when Dale married Shiela. "I, Dale, take you to be my wedded wife," he had vowed in the wedding where I was a guest. "But I also take your son, Carl, to be my son." It was a delightful but heavy and surprising moment to me. There stood Carl as the ring-bearer, five years old, his natural father lost in the drug culture. Two years later I visited the little family. Carl seemed anxious. While he was out of the room, I asked Dale, "Do you cuddle him much?"

"It's not easy to cuddle him when I have to be getting

after him so much of the time," Dale said. Carl, it turned out, was diagnosed as hyperactive, was dyslectic, and was having nightmares in which his new daddy was being killed. "That one doesn't take 'Joseph in Egypt' to get an interpretation," I responded. "It is clear that he has lost one daddy and is afraid he is going to lose another."

I then outlined a program. "What morning of the week can you and Shiela sleep in?" And then, "Do you watch the six-o'clock news in the evening?" I suggested that they haul Carl right into bed, between the two of them for Saturday-morning hugging. "Ten minutes before making the bed would do it," I said. "And get Carl up under your arm and snuggled right close to your body for thirty minutes during the TV news—every day." Amazingly, within a year all three problems had virtually disappeared. Humans must have significant touch to survive and to thrive. Touch and affirmation are the midwives for ushering in any family's peaceable kingdom.

"Behavior modification," a learning model based almost entirely on animal research, will not solve all of our complex questions as human parents. But behaviorism poses three foundational rules which constitute a primer or a first test in parent-child relationships:

1. If you want to increase the frequency of any behavior, follow it by something pleasant.
2. If you want to decrease the frequency, ignore it—or follow it, if you must, by something mildly unpleasant.
3. Avoid punishment because (a) the effects are unpredictable and (b) they are potentially more troublesome than the behavior you are trying to extinguish.

"Punishment" is punitive action directed toward the child's past misdeeds. "Discipline," on the other hand is action focused on improving the child's future behavior. All parents are eager to focus on future behavior. Because of this longing for effective parental responsibility, it becomes urgent that the primary transactions between parent and child be affirming and constructive. The essential correction and discipline need to be mild and minor when compared to the total parent exchanges.

Studies in child abuse show that premature babies are among the highest risk groups—those most likely to be abused. Typically, there is no bonding time with the premature infant because of the life-threatening conditions and the need to get the child to intensive care.

The effects of spontaneous parent-infant exchanges in the first few hours of life, then, are long-term attachment which sets up the foundation for lifelong growth in mutual respect. But extended years of the same intimate behaviors—touching, eye-to-eye contact, for example—tend to enhance parent-child relationships quite beyond or even apart from birth-bonding time. The peaceable kingdom of the family tends to be brought in by small but spontaneous gestures of respect and affection.

### Jesus, Mary, and Joseph

At Texas Tech University's Wesley Foundation, I had wrapped up a session on "sex-role development" by citing the importance of Joseph in the childhood and adolescent development of Jesus. I had projected a transparency showing the text of Matthew 1:18-25. Then I had traced Joseph's uneasy reasoning, all revolving around the troublesome question: "What shall I do with the baby?" It was easy to crack the text to see that his first response was calculated to protect his own public reputation: "I'll get rid of the baby." But then, I said, God had a better idea: "Marry the baby's mother!" because every baby needs a daddy. Finally, the text concluded: "Give the baby a name." I showed that Joseph did, in fact, give the baby the name Jesus, but that the legal record just a few lines ahead of the story indicated that in the official genealogical files, Jesus was the legal son of Joseph. I made the point that the genetic connection was irrelevant. I even cited the words of the anonymous poster:

> I did not plant you true,
> But when the season is done,
> When the alternate prayers for
>     sun and for rain are counted,

When the pain of weeding and
the pride of watching are through,
Then I will hold you high,
a shining sheaf above the
thousand seeds grown wild.
Not my planting,
But my heaven, my harvest,
My child.

I told how I thought I understood the passage. Then, when I had closed my Bible early one Advent season, it hit me. Joseph gave Jesus his own identity, his legal inheritance, and the warmth of parental discipline and affection. But the proof of Joseph's effective father care lies in the fact that Jesus gave God a new name. After centuries in which God had been named Elohim, Jehovah, Yahweh, El Shaddai, and Adonai, God became at last "our Father," even "Abba" or "Daddy Father." And where did Jesus learn the meaning of those primal syllables? It is the highest tribute that Jesus could have paid to Joseph. It is the ultimate "payoff" to fatherhood.

So, the Parent of Eden who loved to walk with the children in the cool of the day has entered our awareness through the last Adam and has renewed the intimate-parent image. The distancing of the centuries had vaulted God to regal and remote positions. The Israelites had demanded a king and in that pagan appetite moved themselves further into a serf-king relationship to their God. Whole theological systems, themselves conceived in monarchial environments, have missed the intimacy of Eden and of Nazareth and have given us hierarchical sovereign theologies. It is as if Bethlehem, Nazareth, and Calvary have brought us all "home again."

When I had finished my talk, a young coed at Tech approached me to say, "Did you know that Jesus was birth-bonded?" I asked what had prompted her conclusion. "Because, you know the nativity hymn says it—" . . . 'the little Lord Jesus, no crying he makes.' And we mused over the uncanny timing of Jesus' birth, including the necessity that he be born in the stable.

Imagine how much of human destiny hung on the special

arrangements by which Mary and Joseph would be denied traditional guest space in Bethlehem. If they had been inside the inn, or had been back home in Nazareth, a midwife's crew would have driven Joseph out of the house while they did "women's work." It is little wonder that the now-famous Search Report of 1984 is documenting that today's teens feel closer to their parents and rely more on them for advice and wisdom than any previous generation that has been studied. The birthing procedures have changed dramatically in the last twenty years. Many fathers go through complete birthing instruction and stay with their spouses through the entire siege of labor, delivery, and birth bonding. We can sing some new songs today about well-bonded babies, the peaceable kingdom, and "the little Lord Jesus, no crying he makes."

## QUESTIONS PEOPLE ASK

*Q: You speak as if birth bonding is really important in establishing the parent-child relationship. Isn't that over-simplified?*

A: There are, no doubt, exceptions. But there is simple physiology at work here, and the human gifts for early attachment appear to be very strong. Birth bonding is not a substitute for long-term intimate care for the child, but it is a fine beginning for the parent-child relationship. And the evidence suggests that birth bonding is likely to evoke improved parental behavior toward the child.

*Q: I feel terrible because our children were, as you say, drawn from me with forceps while I lay under deep anesthesia. I would be happier today if I had never heard anything about birth bonding, because my children are all grown and away from home.*

A: Join the club. Most of us above twenty years of age are from that barbarian birthing era. For most of us, our parents compensated for the wasted early hours by loving us twice as much and through a lot of our rebellion. But rejoice, too, for your grandchildren who may be arriving on this planet under conditions that will assure them they are "home." Spread the good news and urge your daughters and granddaughters to consult with their physicians about having the first two and a half hours for birth bonding with their babies.

*Q: I've never heard of a birth-bonding time in any of our delivery room facilities here. How would we go about finding a place that would permit such a thing?*

A: Begin with your physician. Physicians are able to arrange for birth-bonding time in many hospitals. The procedure is not likely to be promoted by the hospital because of the extra concern such an "irregular procedure" provokes for the staff. If your physician reports that he is unable to make such an arrangement, you will have to decide how important it is to you to find a suitable delivery room. Most physicians will be able to refer patients to other systems if birth-bonding time is a high priority. And most physicians are now aware of the research on birth bonding. If yours seems not to be well grounded on the effects, give him or her the list of citations in the notes on this chapter. Some of these sources are written entirely from a medical perspective.

# 7

# Parents and Children: For Each Other

△

At a Georgia family camp I was just concluding five days of teaching on the family as God's "first curriculum." During that time I had been invited to several family cottages for lunch or late night coffee. Early in the week I had been in the Ambrose house—so early in the week, in fact, that I had trouble figuring out which were the members of the host family in the mix of friends invited in for the hour. Finally I nailed down Jimmy—6'2" and the obvious "eldest" hope of the family's athletic fortunes. His sister, Jill, was six years younger, just turning thirteen.

Since it was an intergenerational family camp, Jimmy and Jill were in all of the same morning sessions that their parents, James and Jennifer, attended. The emcee had announced on Saturday morning that I would be departing for the airport immediately after the morning class. A line formed as I was putting transparencies and folders into my travel case. James Ambrose was in the line.

"I want to thank you for this week," James said. "I was either a 'Fonzie' or a 'Peter Pan' in high school and beyond. I was into cars and girls and drinking and obscene talk. But I have worried about Jimmy, because he never seems to have to be out at night, on the street, in the car, or

122

anything. I have been afraid that he's abnormal. Now you've helped me to see that I am the one who was messed up. I was converted before Jimmy was born, trained for pastoral ministry, and Jimmy has never known anything but a peaceable Christian home. Thank you for helping me to see how different Jimmy is from me, and that *he* is the healthy one."

I quickly folded my case and headed for the guest room. But I was intercepted before I quite got to the building from which I was to be whisked to the Atlanta airport. It was Jennifer.

"I know you are in a hurry, but I just have to tell you something. You explained how girls feel whose fathers don't affirm them, you know? Well, when you talked about 'father absence,' you were describing me. Only, my father wasn't absent, actually. He was a bishop and was gone most of the time. And when he was at home, he seemed distracted, and I have no memory of his ever telling me I was pretty or anything like I needed. You have helped me to understand the kind of vacuum I was feeling and why I was attracted to James and was so vulnerable to his wild lifestyle. I was pregnant with Jimmy when we were married, but both James and I were converted before Jimmy was born. But I was one of those father-absent girls you described. My father might as well have run off or have been dead, so far as I was concerned."

## What a Mother and a Father Do for a Baby

Mothers are "encompassers." Even during delivery, the mother instinctively reaches out to receive and hold the baby to herself. This instinctive behavior is thought to be stimulated by the odor of the placenta with its lanolin lining, and other women present for the delivery sometimes report similar impulses to grasp and hold. Pictures of the Madonna consistently portray Mary holding Jesus to her left breast. This instinctual posturing places the baby nearest the heart of the mother and the soothing sounds of the prenatal chamber.

Fathers are "engrossers." In the delivery room or at other first contact with their infants, fathers usually try to hold the baby in the encompassing position. But they tend to find this uncomfortable, partly because the typical male body is more rigid because of its bone structure and has more than twice as much musculature as the woman. The awkwardness of holding a baby's head on the hard and rounded upper lower arm tends to evoke the father's moving the baby to *en face* positioning: head in cupped hands, looking into the infant's eyes.

Now we might think that it is "nice" that mothers and fathers hold their babies differently. But it may be the first signal the baby receives from the "image of God" represented in its male and female modes. And there will be a lifelong double-image imprint between the child and the two distinctly different parents.

The female side of God's image consistently and powerfully marks the child by its warmth, intimacy, and constant attachment and care. The literal umbilical attachment tends to continue in a psychological attachment; mothering is borderline connectedness throughout life. In the early years the child imagines itself to be an extension of the mother. It ventures out from the mother as "center" and runs back to her as "safety."

In an equally unexpected way, the male side of God's image marks the child by its gift of independence, by its detachment, and by its predictable but undulating patterns of intimacy. Fathers—no doubt partly because they are detached from the actual incubation of the child—tend not to have the psychological umbilical attachment that mothers have. "Your child may not be ready to walk to school alone, but mine is!" is a typical exchange between the father to the mother. Fathers tend to leave the child in the care of the mother or other specialists, only to return on schedule to whisk the child away from the caretaker or mother and to indulge in father-play and care. This intermittent or undulating presence evokes in the child a sense that "the climate has changed" now that Daddy is here.

That father imprint is nowhere more visible than in the play activity which he initiates. Before the first year is out, the father will first elevate the baby—still face to face, as most father play will be—then will throw the baby in the air, careful to catch the baby in the downswing. It now emerges that the inner ear of the human requires exactly this kind of turbulence at the exact time schedule that fathers instinctually throw the child. If the inner ear does not experience such disequilibrium during this sensitive developmental period, the child will tend to experience motion sickness as an adult.

A similar instinctual play pattern emerges when the child is in the toddler phase. Fathers, even those who grew up without fathers of their own, will be inclined toward floor play with the child and will invent wild animal pursuit games. These rough-and-tumble activities tend to persist across several years, often initiated by the child after the appetite for them has developed.

Notice that the father's *en face* elevation, throwing, and wild animal episodes, along with circular swinging play activities, have one thing in common: the father is the "cause" of sensations which evoke both fear and pleasure, simultaneously. This "external," "wholly other," omnipotent, potentially violent and powerful parent has become the source of evoking the mixed emotions of fear and pleasure.

In *The Lion, the Witch, and the Wardrobe,* C. S. Lewis introduces the British children to the wonders of the fantasy world of Narnia.[1] Aslan the Lion is the only hope of returning Narnia to its original and beautiful state; the White Witch has turned it into a tragically cold place where "it is always winter but never Christmas." Aslan is Jesus in symbol.

It is Mr. Beaver who expands the children's understanding about who Aslan really is. Susan wants to know if they will really get to see him and whether Aslan is a man.

"Aslan a man!" Mr. Beaver retorts. "Certainly not." Then he explains the wonders of Aslan, ending with the startling news, "Don't you know who is the King of Beasts? Aslan is a lion—the Lion, the great Lion."

"Ooh!" Susan shivers, "I thought he was a man. Is he— quite safe? I shall feel rather nervous about meeting a lion."

Susan is assured that all people have a problem with their knees' knocking when they meet Aslan. "Then he isn't safe?" she says.

"Safe?" Mr. Beaver's patience wears thin. "Who said anything about safe? 'Course he isn't safe. But he's good."

In a very similar way, children tend to experience their fathers. Fathers are gifted with loud voices, strong musculature, and they appear out of nowhere and seem to have power to change arrangements any way they like—even to taking the child from its mother. Fathers, simply by doing the spontaneous parental things they instinctually want to do, represent God's all-powerful, mighty intervention. They point the child to the One who, above all others, "is not safe, but he is good."

Mothers, on the other hand, represent the unfailing attachment of God, the persistent love and always-present care. The mother points to the One whose "steadfast love endures forever."

It is not surprising that children who suffer interference in their experiences with either their father or their mother tend to form defective views of God. When, for example, I meet some person in his or her teens or twenties who says to me, "I don't think I believe in God anymore," I say, "Tell me about your daddy." And when the young person complains, "Jesus is okay, and I can work with a campus ministry, I think, but I don't think I can ever join a church, and I could never work as a minister in a church," I ask, "Tell me about your mother." Atheism or agnosticism seems most often to be rooted in the father relationship or its absence. But the ability to trust relationships and to make commitments and covenants appears to be rooted in the mother connection.

### Conscience Formation

The early years provide the curriculum for children to acquire internal control—conscience. While there are many factors which feed into conscience, it becomes clear that both parents play significant roles. Here are some of the threads that weave together:

*Admiration.* There is some evidence that infants have no self-consciousness. When Jean Piaget calls this "egocentricism," it sounds like a contradiction. Piaget does not mean that the child is an egomaniac, but that the child is unaware of its own existence and cannot imagine any other perspective but its own. What is more, when the child is old enough to draw stick figures, if you ask for a drawing of "our family," it is fairly typical that the child will draw images of everyone but itself. Robbie and I were guests in a home. The father and host suggested to five-year-old Bobby that he put chairs up to the table and set out plates. With four guests and a family of four, there were to be eight places. But Bobby finished the table with seven. His father asked him to name who was to sit at each place. "Who did you forget?" he asked. The boy carefully pointed around the two rooms in which we were spread, and announced that there was a chair for each person. It was with a great shock that Bobby was shown that he had forgotten himself.

It is out of this unselfconscious egocentricism that the child develops the enormous admiration and respect for the parents. They are the child's "self." Whatever gifts, status, or skills they exhibit belong to the child, exist for the child. It is this uncontaminated unselfconsciousness which Jesus seems to hold out to self-centered adults as the ticket into his kingdom: become as little children. Let your desires and your identity become fixed on God, as children's desires are fixed on the existence and identity of their parents. Accordingly, the young child believes the parents can do no wrong. Anything they do is the best thing on earth to do. Jason, at two, is eager to go with me to work in the yard. I remove my hairpiece. Jason takes his hair by the front lock. "Jason take off his hair," he says softly. I comment, "If you do, I think it will hurt." To which he replies, "Jason play like it." I agree. Then he stings me: "When Jason is a Papaw, he can take his hair off." Piaget calls this "unilateral respect," and it sets up the fertile soil in which the parent is able both to shape the child's sexual identity and to provide experiences by which the child's resistance to temptation will be strengthened.

*Sex identity and sex role.* It is not at all clear how the child establishes its own sexual identity. I use the term sexual *identity* to refer to the inner feelings of any person, by which that person can say or own the fact that "I feel like a male," or "I feel like a female." I use the term *sex role* to refer to the message any person broadcasts to the outside world: "I want you to think of me as a male," or "I want you to think of me as a female." Almost always, sexual identity and sex role agree, and they are grounded in actual biological fact. It is typical that an infant expresses sex-identity preferences long before speech appears. Day-care and nursery operations that hold as any priority the "image of God" concerns for children, will employ staff members of both sexes. And they may be surprised that very young children have distinct sex preferences for custodial care. Parents see the preferences in early "imitation play." The child will want to do "mother things" or "father things." From time to time, I have offered my six grandchildren my electric razor, as one of them would join me to watch the operation. Each of the three boys has held still for me to move the buzzing but harmless side over his little face. Not one of the girls has been willing for me to stroke her face with the shaver. Robbie faced a line-up of four of the children one evening. She was dispensing Rose Milk for the hands and face. Jason stood in the line-up with the three granddaughters. Robbie turned to him last, "Do you want some?" "No way!" was the disgusted response of a seven-year-old nicely sex-typed male.

Jordan, at four years, was making his first visit to his great grandparents' farm in Kansas. He was in the car with us for two days enroute from Kentucky, with an overnight in Columbia, Missouri. We had visited the famous Arch in St. Louis, had lunch on the McDonald's Riverboat nearby, and had the usual number of stops along the way. Within five minutes of our arrival, my mother asked Jordan what he wanted to be when he grew up. "A grandpa, so I can be bossy," was his instant, unreflected reply. My concern for his safety every time we left the car and my eagerness for him to keep his feet off the seat until his shoes were removed had portrayed a male role of some significant authority which he found appealing. I was embarrassed, but it was wasted on him. That is exactly what he aspired to be.

It is not difficult to see that these examples illustrate how the inner feelings of the children matched the outward broadcast messages about their sexuality. The examples also show how "significant" adults become the models—what the parent does is regarded as a sex-appropriate thing to do. This powerful lever in the hands of the parent sets up the scene for experiences in which the child will develop the capacity to control its appetites and desires.

*Delay of gratification.* Virtually all of the so-called sins of youth are rooted in what Robert Sears has called "delay of gratification."[2] At Stanford University, Dr. Sears has developed what he calls "resistance-to-temptation tests." When children do not develop the ability to wait—to delay gratification—we can see criminal behavior in adolescence and adulthood. Thus, steal if you cannot wait until you can come by the money necessary to purchase an object. Drink before the legal age, if you must establish your validity as an adult before that age. Sleep with your friend, if you cannot wait until the wedding night. All of these troublesome behaviors have delay of gratification as a single common denominator.

Watch how the parent or any important adult is able to use the gifts of the adult-child relationship to strengthen the child's ability to wait. The pattern runs like this:

1. Child wants something very much.
2. Adult is the admired source/resource controlling delivery.
3. Adult intervenes, places desire "on hold," with explanation.
4. Child is frustrated, but trusts the adult.
5. Adult "delivers" as promised.

At twenty-two months, Jason was to be the weekend guest at our house. With our six grandchildren living within twenty minutes of our home, the visits are frequent and they have never regarded our house as "being away from home," but rather as an extension of home. John and Julie, Jason's parents, were enrolled in Marriage Enrichment for the weekend, and we had a trip to Nashville with one of my classes. Our trip was to end at noon on Saturday, so the great grandparents took Jason for Friday night until we would pick him up.

We arrived at the Bowles' home an hour after noon on Saturday. We had decided to fast at lunch time in order to make the trip a little shorter. At the door we were met by a very excited Jason. He slipped through great-grandparent legs and onto the porch. There he tugged and shook my trousers. Promised excitement had arrived for him. "Go in Papaw's big car; go in Papaw's big car," were his high-demand words. But Robbie and I were being offered cake and ice cream. I scooped Jason into my arms and announced: "We'll go in the car, but first we are going to have some cake and ice cream." That seemed acceptable to Jason, and I put him back down on the floor. We proceeded with adult conversation and the dessert. At some point Jason crawled up onto my lap. I was unaware of him, largely ignoring him, until I realized that I had a faceful of hair for my final bites of cake. But I simply leaned around him to eat. He was not sitting sideways or *en face,* as I would normally have held him. It was not until the last bite was airborne that I realized why he was on my lap at all. He was monitoring my promise. And with the cake in the air on my fork, two small hands came over the side of the table, shoving the plate to the center, and Jason announced, "All through! Now go in Papaw's big car."

"You are right," I announced and rose to leave. Once in the car, I tantalized him further, all without thinking of the delay-of-gratification pattern in all of this. "Do you know what I am going to do when we get home?" I asked. He was total attention. "I'm going to get out the lawn mower and the tractor and we are going to work in the yard." This meant that he could wear the special cap which I keep for him to wear, and we would be partners. He was ecstatic. Once there, he ran toward the tool shed, stopping fifty yards away to call to me, "Papaw! Lawn mower! Tractor!"

I had not intended to set up such an immediate strong desire. "I have to change my clothes," I said. "Look at me, I can't work now. And you're wet, you have to have a clean diaper." When I arrived at the house, he had retreated and was waiting there for me. Evidently I had intercepted his desire, frustrating it with a necessary reason for waiting. It took me some time to unpack the suitcases, and I don't know what he may have been doing during that time. I next became aware of him as I was standing in the walk-in closet, changing into my working clothes. Over my shoulder I caught a glimpse of Jason. He was lying on his back, spread-eagled on a plastic rug where his diaper had been changed dozens of times. He was willing to pay the price of that inconvenience because he wanted so much to work with Papaw. Never before in our experience with him had a diaper change come at his initiative, but I had made it part of the prerequisite to his desire, and he was here to have the operation completed.

*Saturation.* Parent-child experiences like mine with Jason occur every day. It takes about ten years, plus or minus two, to bring the child to reasonable freedom and responsibility. By the time of the onset of pubescence, such character is important, since the parent is largely shut out of the inner dynamic of the child by the necessary privacy which is ushered in by sexual maturity. Most exchanges that strengthen the conscience will go unnoticed. It was a week or more before I was aware of the pressure cooker I had provided for Jason in the space of half an hour of normal grandparent-child experience. Two criteria are critical, but if they are present, you can be sure that positive delay of gratification is occurring:

1. Positive emotion from parent toward child, matches child's attraction to parent.
2. Highly verbal exchanges; everything responded to, and everything explained, including delays.

It looks so simple when reduced to a formula, yet thereby the "image of God" is imprinted on the child, and the resistance to temptation is strengthened. In Dr. Sears' studies it became clear that the warmth and affection of the father was a variable which seemed always to be high in the cases of boys who could resist temptation. The RTT tests, as they were called, typically placed the child in a room with some dull toys and with a bowl of candy which was "not ours," according to the adult who was working with the child. When the adult was called from the room, leaving the child alone under the scrutiny of researchers behind one-way glass, the child's strength of conscience was measured by minutes and seconds. Girls with strong identification with their mothers scored high, as did boys whose fathers played wild-animal games with them on the living room rug. When we look at the parent-child relationship, it is clear, as Dr. Sears says: "The responsibility for the conscience lies directly in the hands of the parents."

Heather bounded out of her sleeping bag at the first sounds of Grandma's Saturday morning routine: "What are we going to have for breakfast?" "I thought we would have biscuits and gravy," Grandma said. "How do you make gravy?" was Heather's response.

Robbie sat Heather up on the kitchen countertop, where she could watch the entire operation: "You watch me, and I'll show you how I make gravy." With hands on hips, intensely focused on mastering the art of gravy-making, Heather summed up her motivation: "Someday, I'm going to have to make gravy." The adult images in the eyes of a child filled with unilateral respect provide the magically shaping force in the young child's development. It is simply by "being a mother" and by taking pleasure in contact with the child that the foundation is laid.

## The Final Touch

In those first years, which I call "up until age ten, plus or minus two," the child tends to send out a unilateral respect signal to the parent of the same sex that says: "I will copy you in everything you do, because you can only do 'good' in my eyes." The signal beamed out to the parent of the opposite sex also has much imitation in it, but there is an additional signal: "You are different from me, so I will learn how to relate to you from the opposite perspective."

I worried when Mike played so wildly with Heather, his firstborn. It was clear that he was ready to roughhouse with a boy, but Heather was getting the first full load of his father-play. "Be careful," I warned him, "or you will make a 'tom boy' out of her." I need not have worried. Now, nearly seven years later, she is distinctly the most feminine of the three granddaughters. Mike's playfulness was evidently always regarded as masculine, and as opposite to her own emerging femininity. It seems likely that no healthy child can be thrown off balance in his or her developing sexual identity and sex role—what I have called, in combination, "sex-role typing"—so long as both parents are present and active in the child's life. The child evidently picks up, instinctually, the correct package of sex-appropriate behaviors and responds to the opposite parent in a way which only accents the sex-appropriate expressions. Think of the photographic film-developing process. It is as if the same-sex parent brings up the film in a "positive image" with a look-alike pattern, while the parent of the opposite sex brings up a "negative image," with its reverse density and tone. Both are essential if the child is to be fully formed in sex-role typing.

With the onset of pubescence—following the magic age of ten plus or minus two—the emerging adolescent tends to depend upon the opposite sex parent for what I call "the final touch." You will recognize the pattern:

1. Teen appears to become self-aware; spends a lot of time dealing with the image in the mirror.
2. Teen tends to "consult" with opposite sex parent about social performance; may seem indifferent or even hostile to same-sex parent.
3. Teen hangs on words and non-verbal signals of acceptance or rejection by opposite-sex parent.

The message which the emerging adolescent seems to be giving is this: *"I am about to be an adult. I have to know whether I can make it on my own. What I need is coaching from an expert who can make valid, objective judgments about my acceptability in the larger world in which I must move."*

We can expect that the adolescent will become anxious,

even violent, if the opposite-sex parent gives primarily negative feedback or withholds affirmation and gives nonverbal signals of rejection. But an affirming opposite-sex parent tends to become the midwife to adulthood for the teenager, and has almost unlimited privileges in sculpting the form and character of the child-becoming-an-adult.

Therefore, it is typical, and an occasion for rejoicing, when a young man consults his mother about shaving lotion, clothes, hairstyle or treatment, telephone protocol, how to get a date, and whether he said or did the right thing. Anyone knows that it is the father who considers himself the authority on all of these matters—but it is the mother who is the "experienced consumer" of male behaviors. And it is the mother who can also drop hints which compare the son to the father—a secret piece of information the young man yearns for, since he is nervous that he may be clumsy and inept by comparison at the same age. Mother will tell. She will also give personal evaluation: "I was born twenty years too soon," she may say. The mother has almost unlimited opportunity to give final polish and shape to her young son.

It is equally typical and healthy when the emerging young woman seeks out the advice of her father on acceptability of a choice of clothing, hairstyle, perfume, makeup, how to say yes or no when asked for a date. Again, these are matters on which the mother is the resident expert, but Dad holds the exclusive patent on these "consumer" perspectives—and Dad is safe. So the father who wishes to "safe-proof" his daughter does everyone a favor to tell her she is pretty and stunning, and give her the impression that any date is lucky if she says yes to an evening out. She also gets another message: I will have to answer to Daddy; and my friend will have to meet his approval, too.

On one occasion a distressed father negotiated with his wife and daughter, then invited me to fly in to work for healing in a family "fracture" over the daughter's engagement to a young man who was unacceptable to either the father or the mother. I told them that I was "not in the business" of breaking up engagements, but that if Mary, the daughter, would phone me herself, I would come. During an evening session with the parents, John and Betty, I learned that Betty had forbidden Mary to come home again until "she gets rid of that awful boyfriend." I probed at Mary's relationship to Betty in early childhood. Mary had been the perfect daughter, it seemed. "We did everything together," Betty said. "But then something happened, and Mary turned to her father."

I watched the accusation shoot across the room. It was motivated by enough energy to carry a charge of father incest, but I doubted the probability, since no other symptoms were evident. So, I explained about the "final polish," and how a daughter is lucky to have a dad who affirms her when she hits junior high school. I saw Betty wipe her eyes. "You mean it is supposed to be that way—that I would have to give Mary up just when she got grown?"

"It is not inevitable, and sometimes it happens without a lot of pain, but yes," I said, "it often has some pain in it."

"I can tell you the day it happened," Betty said. "Mary and I had spent most of the day shopping downtown Denver. Mary was in eighth grade and needed her first formal. We finally found one that seemed right. When Mary heard her dad's car in the driveway, she ran to her room, got the dress in its box, and met him at the door. He said simply, 'I don't want to see it in a box. Put it on.' Mary was gone for a few minutes. Then, from the kitchen, I watched as she modeled it in the living room. John circled her, doing a 'wolf whistle,' and saying, 'I can't believe this. When did you grow up? You're beautiful. My baby is a woman!' That is the day I lost my daughter, and you are telling me it was supposed to be that way."

"Well," I said, "Mary is a lucky girl to have a father who gives her that kind of high rating as a woman." I was to learn from Mary that John secretly phoned her several times a week, and was unable to abide by Betty's "shunning" policy. It was the father's attachment to the daughter that had sustained her through the months of expulsion from the home. I was able to say to Betty, "Whatever else happens this weekend, I want to tell you that you must lift the ban and let Mary come home again. If you do not, then you are starving her for her father's affirmation. You can be sure that the young man at the university is ready, willing, and able to affirm her, and you may be the person most responsible for her quick marriage if you shut her away from home just now."

Sometimes the opposite-sex parent is unable to provide the affirmation the adolescent needs. This is often true if the parental marriage is unstable. And in the event of divorce, the father's affirmation for the daughter is seriously jeopardized, of course. But the affirmation may also be frozen up if the parent is suffering from depression, anxiety, or serious feelings of insecurity. A healthy parent needs to rather like being forty or more, enjoy parent-child exchanges, and be ready to serve as that midwife who delivers freedom and responsibility to the child right on schedule. The healthy parent will be affectionate in the marriage relationship, and that will be obvious to the teen. When the child becomes socially active, the parental marriage is the inevitable model on which the emerging young adult is constructing relationships. A boy's best assurance that his mother knows what she is talking about is found in the obviously strong, affectionate marriage the young man observes in his parents. And a girl's surest foundation for safety in the whole world is found in the clear evidence that her father truly loves and respects her mother. If her father is frozen up in his marriage, he is likely either to: (a) be frozen up toward her developing sexuality, fear it, even sense his own arousal toward her; or (b) be sexually dangerous to her. If the father exploits the daughter when she needs truly safe affirmation, he drives her quickly out of the home and into the arms of some man who will deliver her from the exploitive environment. That deliverer is very likely to be someone who has won her through competitive exploitation.

## The Broken Image

If we agree that every child needs both a father and a mother to imprint the full-spectrum image of God, then loss of either side of the image must be regarded as a major tragedy. We will not be surprised to note that there are critical periods in early life when a child needs one parent more than another:

1. From birth to age ten, the same-sex parent provides the model for sex-typing.
2. From ten to twenty, the opposite-sex parent provides the "final polish" for adult launching.
3. Even in the "off season" phase, the parent provides the stable marriage and loving foundation for the top-priority parent to do the urgent work.

Since the close of World War II, some research attention has been given to "father absence."[3] The first studies were triggered by unusual patterns in test scores of entering college students. Follow-up studies disclosed that the pattern matched the absence of fathers who were away in military service for extended periods of time. Young male college students who had been essentially without fathers for several months showed lower scores, in general, on math and higher scores on verbal ability than did those whose fathers were continuously in the home.

The divorce rate since World War II has continued to separate children from natural fathers.[4] Mothers, typically, are assigned custody of children, and women who lose their husbands either through death or divorce tend not to remarry at the relatively high rate characteristic of men. For this reason, children are only rarely separated from the natural mother, and no comparable research sample has been identified to study the effects of "mother absence."

The research on father absence since 1954 has continued to become more and more sophisticated, and some studies separate the patterns of effects on the basis of whether the absence was caused by death or by desertion and divorce. The pattern unfolds with different effects for boys and for girls:

*The Fonzie Club.* Boys without fathers tend to display symptoms seen less often in father-present sons: (a) defective sex-role typing, passivity versus compensatory masculinity; (b) low numerical and higher verbal scores on college entrance exams; (c) defective conscience control; and (d) sexual inversion.

Defective sex-role typing is visible in two distortions. The passive male, often introverted, lacks confidence for dealing with the social world. It is as if he has missed the basic course in how to deal with people in the mixed world of males and females. In my own observation, this is complicated even more when the entire remaining household is female. And the critical period for sex-role typing, remember, is during the first ten years of life. Boys who lose their fathers after the age of eight or ten tend not to suffer from passive sex-role typing. On the other hand, more assertive young boys and many teenaged boys indulge in what researchers call "compensatory masculinity."

These standard Fonzie types tend to be assertive, often extroverted, lack father attention, often act out macho behavior. Fonzies pick up small fragments of male behaviors which they exaggerate: hard talking, hard consuming, smoking, drinking, and wild driving macho behavior. They tend to regard women as objects to be used and abandoned, but frequently find in the affirmation of a woman the security they need to enter the more normal part of the human race. These compensatory-masculinity actions are gestures calculated to prove one's manhood. As such, the macho male is the most insecure of all types. Reading disabilities abound in these males, as do low numerical scores. They suffer from defective conscience control, as is evident by the frequent encounters with police and the courts. They tend to be preoccupied with motor-driven vehicles, which they seem to use as extensions of their sexuality. The motorcycle or car is often altered to capture public and law-enforcement attention, especially as it is usually modified to exaggerate the noise it produces. A van is typically outfitted to be an obvious "rolling bedroom," with exaggerated symbols of sexual prowess decorating the vehicle.

The Fonzie TV character plays out the well-researched pattern of the father-absent male, and he does so within the bounds of discretion suitable for public consumption. It is easy to see that early father absence deprives a boy of basic skills in how to treat a woman, how to show respect and affection to a woman, and how to establish an intimate and lifelong bond with a woman. The special efforts of a mother might yet tame Fonzie as he enters adolescence, especially if the boy has had access to his natural father or a positive surrogate/substitute father in the early months and years of his life.

Implications for the larger community are clear. Boys without fathers need both male and female child-care attendants, and church staffing of classes and clubs should include both males and females. A mother rearing a young son alone may want to establish close ties with her larger family and negotiate extensive time from her brother, father, or other male relative to spend with her son. There is evidence that boys are quite able to establish ties with safe and healthy males from the school, church, or community. However, with the increasingly anonymous communities in which we live, such relationships must more often now be deliberately sought out and contracted, even among friends.

Sexual inversion, or homosexual preference and practice, tends to occur more often among males whose fathering has been interrupted. While this is not surprising when one thinks of the passive, mother-smothered son, it tends also to show up in the Fonzie or macho types. Among these more assertive males, the inversion sometimes takes the form of "gang rape" of a weaker, smaller, and/or more passive male. These same macho types would no doubt march on a "gay caucus" meeting with violence, and would never associate this homosexual aggression with sexual inversion. Their heavy reliance on sexually explicit language as put-downs or their use of hand signals denoting sexual intercourse to execute the ultimate, violent put down on the highway, exposes their deep sexual confusion. They regard their sexuality as a means of expressing violence, and they have never learned the language or the gestures of affection.

*The Peter Pan Syndrome,* a recent book by Dr. Dan Kiley, describes the confusion of sex-typing in sons when parent relationships are disturbed.[5] While Kiley does not address father absence, he does show that emotionally deformed fathers and mothers can paralyze the young son's emerging masculinity. He uses the Peter Pan designation to evoke the image of that famous character who cannot face the responsibilities of becoming a man. It is not surprising, Kiley notes, that in the typical stage production of *Peter Pan*, the central character is played by a young woman. Typically, there are several forces at work, which cause a young male to reject full adult male responsibilities. The *Playboy* culture is essentially a whole population of Peter Pan characters by Kiley's criteria: They want freedom, but reject responsibility. They want pleasure, but reject pain. They want the symbols of success, but reject the means of achievement. They want affluence, but lack the restraint to earn their own riches.

Here is Kiley's list of characteristics of the Peter Pan. In the book, these factors are arranged into a "test" with a "score" to identify how strong is one's tendency toward Peter Pan:

| | | |
|---|---|---|
| Flirts | Doesn't listen | Flashes of rage |
| Cold relationships | No foreplay | No feelings ex- |
| Drinking problem | Won't miss fun | pressed |
| Chauvinistic | No apologies | Selfish about outings |
| Helps buddies | Underemployed | Denies having fears |
| Above it all | Nagged to "care" | Intimidated by Mom |
| | Forgets dates | Distant from Dad |

Finally, Dr. Kiley summarizes a particularly tragic set of relationships which tend to develop between a father and a mother to set up the paralysis of the Peter Pan:

| Event | Son's Construction |
|---|---|
| Dad says, "Leave your mother alone, she's not able to handle so much demand. Remember she's the 'weaker sex.' " | Women are weak and have to be shielded from reality. |
| Mom says, "I'm so glad you are not like your father. He never thinks to help me with dishes." | It would be terrible to grow up to be like my father, but that's how men are. |

*The Aldonza Pattern.* Girls without fathers, according to the research on father absence, tend to fall into two general patterns.

1. Girls who have lost the father by death tend to become shy at adolescence.
2. Girls who have lost the father by desertion or divorce, tend to become sexually aggressive.

In either case, two generalizations apply:

3. The severity of the effects are in direct proportion to how early the father left.
4. Both types are vulnerable to sexual seduction, and both tend to relate immaturely to men.

I showed up at a family camp as supervisor of a half-dozen of my students who were to direct the teen program for a week. I had personally met about fifty teens during registration and invited them to sit in a designated area of the camp chapel during evening vespers. It was a humid August night, but the couple who planted themselves just in front of me hugged intimately during the entire hour. Following the benediction, I introduced myself, "I don't think I have met either of you." They smiled shyly and introduced themselves: Roy and Lucy.

"How long have you been dating?" I asked.

"This is our first date," Roy volunteered.

"Wow! You could have fooled me," I said, and we all smiled.

Roy abandoned Lucy immediately after vespers. It turned out that he was all of thirteen years old and she was eighteen, recently graduated from high school. "I wouldn't go out with her again if she was the last woman on earth!" he had confided to his friends—normal-sized twelve- and thirteen-year-olds. The explosion put Lucy in the racks for two days. But after the other women had fed her in the dormitory for two days, she finally came out for lunch. "I want to see you after lunch," I said. "I know you have been embarrassed by what Roy has done."

We sat at the edge of the open-air chapel that afternoon. "I'm really sorry you got hurt," I opened.

"It's okay," she replied. "When I get home from camp there's this guy who is shipping out for Vietnam, and he's going to be home for six weeks. I expect to be pregnant by him before he leaves."

"Oh. You are pretty desperate, Lucy. May I ask you some questions?" I was glad I had recently stumbled on to the father-absent research. It guided my probing and my judging, too.

"Tell me about your dad," I began.

"What's there to tell? He left before I was born. And it's terrible living with Mother. It's like a battlefield, and I've got to get out of the house. If Billy will marry me if I get pregnant, then I'll have an income to get by until he gets home."

Lucy had played out the classical sequence that is typical of girls who lose their fathers by desertion or divorce. These steps of illogical decision making tend to proceed this way:

1. I lost the one man I needed most, my Father.
2. I will replace him; any man will do.
3. The way to trap a man is to get pregnant by him.
4. Even if he won't marry me, maybe I will have a baby boy; then I will raise me a man.

"Tell me, Lucy, do you know a couple in your church back home, maybe a pair who have already reared their family—somebody you respect a lot?" She named a couple. "Now, name another couple, maybe your pastor and his wife?" Then I asked whether she could open her heart to them, tell them how desperate she was. She thought she could. I prayed with this beautiful young woman. I told her, "You are much too fine a woman to settle for just anybody who could spring you out of the house. I can imagine that you could marry the finest man at this camp. So try to dream the best dreams in the world, and let Jesus help bring them to reality for you." Lucy successfully established the "family of God" network she needed, and she continues to work occasionally as a summer-camp volunteer. She also abandoned her get-pregnant-quick scheme for capturing a man.

Aldonza is the flamboyant prostitute in *Man of La Mancha*. Don Quixote falls in love with her, salutes her as "my virgin," and declares that she is essential to his adventure of dreaming "the impossible dream" and winning the world for right and truth and love. But she is a cynical woman who knows that "all men are the same when they are in bed." But Quixote stops her cold, and she almost captures the vision of herself as virginal and innocent again.

I use the "Aldonza pattern" to designate the damaged woman who is the counterpart of Fonzie and of Peter Pan. These girls without fathers—or with abusing, or neglectful, or otherwise dysfunctional fathers—tend to appear quite normal until the onset of pubescence. Then, with the hormonal and the social pressures building, they become aggressive toward males if they are relatively extroverted. The more introverted girls tend simply to send the non-verbal signals of their availability. In either case, they tend to become sexually active earlier and at higher rates than girls with affirming and available fathers. Watch for these symptoms and characteristics:

• Sexually mature young women tend to develop a high need for affirmation and touch—to be "encompassed." They tend to cling and to send a signal to the male that they are sexually available.
• Girls abandoned by desertion or divorce blame themselves: "If I had been worth loving, Daddy would never have left."
• Abandoned girls may be motivated by both loneliness and anger. Some set out to hurt men for belonging to the side of the species that hurt them.
• Father-absent girls tend to lack social skills, especially those needed in relating to males.
• Father-absent girls tend to contribute to a fast-track romance, with a tendency for the pair bond to break from rushing or missing steps.

The good news is that here, as with father-absent boys, stable, available men and couples in the community can, with little effort, shut down the anxiety and help the girls mature gracefully. "When my father and my mother forsake me, then the Lord will take me up" (Ps. 27:10 KJV) was not promised primarily for a heavenly relationship. "The Lord" is the church, Jesus, present and active in the world as both Bride and Groom. This full-spectrum family of God is the most fully resourced agency in the world for calling to "orphans and widows in their affliction" (James 1:27 RSV) "Give me your father-absent children," the community of faith might say, "and we will be additional fathers and mothers to them."

## God Loves Single Parents

"Widows" and "the fatherless" are the special concern of God. You can read it throughout the Old Testament. And James makes the single parent household the acid test of "pure and faultless" Christian faith:

> Religion that God our Father accepts as pure and faultless is this: to look after orphans and widows in their distress and to keep oneself from being polluted by the world.
>
> James 1:27

One prominent pastor told me (I thought a little proudly), "There are no divorced people in our entire congregation." I thought, *"What a tragedy!"* With nearly half of America's children living with only one natural parent, it was clear that his congregation was dangerously out of touch with half of any typical community.

With concern for the poor increasingly falling back onto the shoulders of the private sector, it remains to be seen whether the church becomes a haven for the single-parent household, with its special economic and time problems. Here are some things a congregation or a faith community might do:

1. Provide child care parallel to every adult activity— not simply on Sunday schedules.

2. Run after-school or even before-school programs for children and youth until the parent's (or parents') work schedule permits care and supervision at home. The churches need more educational and playing time with the young. The education ministries might move into these

prime time needs and solve both their own problem and family schedule difficulties. Virtually all dangerous experimentation occurs when children are at home while parents are on a predictable schedule away from the house.

3. Train a significant number from your congregation as surrogate parents. Any of us may be "adopted," by the mystery of God's bonding processes. A child with an emotional need for some extra parent care may be formed "whole" by our special attention and touch. The church is the one agency in which we could expect that such extra-parent care might be available.

4. Facilitate "family clusters" in the congregation, in which both single-parent and intact families are structured together for share-meeting groups where there is a commitment to fellowship, prayer, and mutual concern and support.

5. Staff all ministries with equal numbers of males and females when the children and youth populations include any whose fathers are absent or dysfunctional. The child's need, not our imagination, dictates the time at which a woman is needed and the time when a man is needed. Both must be present if the full-spectrum image is to be complete in our contact with each child.

6. Consider, at least long range, providing a child and adult day-care center. This inter-generational service makes a bold spiritual statement about the need of young for the old and of old for the young. Some ambulatory older adults are well able to provide a few hours of "care" for children, even while they themselves are being cared for by having working-hour supervision.

Since the image-of-God/male-and-female is our "first curriculum," it follows that a corrective or remedial course is essential for those whose curriculum has been interrupted. If we are committed to wholeness in families and congregations, we will eagerly study ways of fulfilling God's concern for the single-parent family.

### Set Them Free

A prominent college president tells how his daughter awakened both parents at one o'clock in the morning.

Standing in the bedroom door she whispered, "Are you awake?"

Any parent will be awake under those circumstances. "What's wrong?" they asked.

"I just wanted to tell you that I broke my engagement tonight," she said. "Bill insisted that I sleep with him tonight, or he said the wedding was off. When I realized that he was dead serious, I told him that I had decided a long time ago that I wasn't going to bed with anybody until my wedding night. If he couldn't accept that, I would have to accept that our relationship was over."

The president muses: "I think I know when Sue developed the capacity to say that 'no.' When she was about eight years old, we took her shopping for a new pair of shoes. After twenty minutes or so, there were three pairs of shoes she liked. She told us to decide which she should have. Her mother and I told her that since she would be the one who was wearing the shoes, we wanted her to make the choice. 'But I can't decide,' she said. So we told her we would do some other shopping in the mall while she decided. Every thirty minutes we would check in. On the third trip, she had made up her mind. I think that was when she developed the strength to make decisions for herself."

All parents know that they are investing in "adult making" when they are living out their lives with children. And nothing is more healthy than for two parents of the opposite sex who form the full-spectrum image of God for the child to consistently develop the child for freedom and responsibility.

When our younger son was sixteen, we sensed a lively streak in him. I had heard horror stories of kids in jail— "one phone call"—and I knew, too, the heavy load that comes from bearing the name and reputation of religious parents, especially famous ones. On one trip Mike made, he was confronted by seat mates three times on this matter. Each of the persons mentioned my name on hearing his: "Are you related?" they would ask. When he told of the encounters, I detected some pride, but it seemed also to be echoing a slight sense of entrapment. So I took him aside.

"Mike, I want you to know that the family name belongs to you. It came to me in pretty good shape. But I don't own it. And there is nothing you can do to it that will devastate us. You are ours and we always want to be right beside you if you need us. But we don't need to control you." We shook hands to seal the deal.

In this chapter I have wanted you to sense the power of the double image in critical events as the child matures. The magic of sex-typing in early childhood moves abruptly into the "final polish" of adolescence. In this dance of parenting, the steps change, and the child's emerging needs are sometimes surprising. And I wanted you to sense that most of us cannot do it alone. We need the community of faith, and we pray that the models and the friends of our children will be healthy and safe, too.

## QUESTIONS PEOPLE ASK

*Q: The Fonzie, Peter Pan, and Aldonza material sounds a little artificial. Aren't these dangerous oversimplifications?*

A: Any generalization may be dangerous. There are splendid exceptions to the clusters to which you object. We all rejoice that specific people escaped "alive and well" from troubled family circumstances. The groupings are helpful only if they match with some regularity to troubled people who are important to us. Since there is some research undergirding the clusters, we are enabled to examine our relationships to those persons and to introduce changes which might prevent the personal deformity from leading to long-term life tragedies.

*Q: What happens when Fonzie or Peter Pan get together with Aldonza? Isn't it likely that they will?*

A: They get together very often; the deformities are custom-made for each other. I have sometimes called these relationships "symbiotic" since they tend to feed off each other and either cluster by itself is parasitic. In *The Prophet*

(*On Marriage*), Kahlil Gibran cautions young lovers, encouraging them to create some "spaces in your togetherness."

> Even as the strings of a lute are alone
> though they quiver with the same music . . . .
> And stand together yet not too near together:
> For the pillars of the temple stand apart,
> And the oak tree and the cypress
> grow not in each other's shadow.[6]

Sometimes, though not often enough to trust it, a union of Fonzie and Aldonza will shock both of them into responsibility and settling down. This is especially true if both experience the mysteries of sexual bonding and Christian conversion about the same time. There are few sources of radical internal change, but repentance, faith in God, and conversion is the one event which *can* transform values and behavior. Young adults moving into the priority of intimacy are unusually vulnerable to such converting grace. Dr. Dan Kiley, author of *The Peter Pan Syndrome*, reported during a Phil Donahue talk show appearance that our age fifteen-to-thirty male population is literally laced with large numbers of males who are refusing to take adult responsibility, the Peter Pans. Although we are pampering boys and turning out Peter Pans, our daughters are very likely to be attracted to these affluent, car-crazy males when they begin to date. We may want to train our young to spot Peter Pan and Fonzie and Aldonza and to empathize with the tragedies behind their extravagant behaviors.[7]

# 8

# *Adolescence: Is There Life After Puberty?*

△

Our house was bracing itself for a typical full evening. Our sons had converged from Jefferson Elementary and Center Ward Junior High. The last touches of our evening meal were being applied. I was still on my feet, when some highly explosive subject emerged between the older son and me. There were quick and hot words, each standing the other off in an adversary position. I knew that I had reacted and that my reaction had evoked the hostile exchange. I stuck out my hand in the gesture of a handshake.

"I'm sorry, John. I've been afraid of what might happen when we get a couple of teenagers around the house. And if this is any sample of the kinds of explosions that may happen, I want to tell you that I couldn't take that. I want you to know right now that I always respect you, and that will be true even if I raise my voice. You are my son, and in all the world, I am committed to you and Mike and Robbie. If I could be sure that you respect me, then I think I can take any of the words you may have to shoot at me."

John mumbled, "Okay," and we shook hands, embraced, and wiped our eyes. There have been some candid exchanges since that day when John was barely thirteen, but neither of us has seriously questioned whether the base of unconditional love remains intact.

## The Physiology of Puberty

The word *pubescence* is from a Latin word which means "to become hairy." We have come to use the term to describe just that period in human development: the two-year period during which the child becomes an adult, or "hairy." Armpits, genital area, and the male face are points on the body marked by increased amounts and different kinds of hair. But there is a good deal more going on than these hair markers alone.

For the emerging young woman there is the typical growth spurt. She often worries that "I'm going to be a giraffe!" Since girls enter pubescence, typically marked by the first menstrual cycle, about one year (or more) ahead of boys, they may be up to twelve inches taller than boys of the same age. Although a girl rarely grows more than one inch in height after her first menstrual period, her height often worries her. Her breasts "bud," and the hips tend to widen. Her fatty tissue stores the estrogens which both motivate her developing womanhood and support her fertility. Infertility in adult females is often a matter of insufficient fatty tissue to hold the estrogen support necessary for fertility. The young woman's primary sex system will mature, the vaginal tract and lips enlarging. And, of course, she will develop the axillary and pubic hair which pubescence denotes.

The emerging young man, like the young woman, will also experience a growth spurt, often growing as much as one inch per month at the crest of the development tide. His entry point may hinge on first ejaculation, often experienced as a "wet dream" in which the overloaded vesicle system explodes spontaneously during the dream cycle at night. More often, however, the enlarging testicles and penis motivate masturbation, fueled by the pleasure sensitivity the young man discovers in the penis. The boy's voice is transformed, typically, in a two-stage voice change. Note that we are still having to transform an essentially female body into that of a male. This will be nowhere more evident than in the slimming of the hips, the loss of "baby fat" from many husky boys. Their shoulders widen, as the body moves to its 40 percent musculature (compared to the 23 percent musculature of the adult woman). Downy facial hair which appears at the onset of pubescence, becomes straight or kinky pigmented hair by the end of the two-year period, and the young man is into shaving or growing facial hair on purpose. Groin, armpit, and chest hair round out the pubescence "hairy" description. Last of all, hair will appear in the ears, but this comes approximately ten years after the onset of pubescence. Curiously, at the age of twenty-three, on the average, the appearance of hair in the ears matches almost exactly the age at which North American males arrive at full adult responsibility.

Both men and women tend to look back to their first sign of sexual maturity as the threshold to adulthood. First menstrual period and first ejaculation are each, in very different ways, held in memory as rites of passage. But the pubescence impact on the brain may be, in fact, the most significant physiological change.

Hormonal chemistry to the brain appears to be related to the awakening of self-consciousness. The sure sign that anybody has entered pubescence is extended time locked in the bathroom. This privacy time tends to be spent before the mirror, partly making peace with the "new body," but also asking a whole new set of questions:

"Who am I, really?"

"Am I worth loving? Will anyone 'want' me forever?"

"What does God want me to do with my life and my energy, especially my sexual feelings?"

"How can I reconcile what I am feeling with what God wants from me?"

We know that the final maturing of the central nervous system is marked by the myelinization of the correlation fibers of the central cortex. The myelin coating on selected parts of the nervous system begins in the infant and progresses slowly to the end of pubescence. This insulation like coating speeds up neurological messages. We see it in eye-hand coordination in the child of six months. When we see the arrival of "reversible thinking," which is essential for making profound moral choices based on thought instead of on experience, we may be witnessing the gift of

God—a pubescent child, charged with sexual energy, is now in possession of a brain which can do reversible, formal thinking, cognitive choosing based on hypothetical evaluation. I have taken the position, elsewhere, that God's design in human growth and development makes adolescence the "crucible for creating saints."[1] The sexual agenda of both young women and young men provides a universal crucial responsibility; and the brain development lets them know that the responsibility lies with them alone. Religious conversion and rebellion are two roads between which the emerging young adult often chooses. Many retain some options for each, leading a double life and accumulating guilt which itself is part of the crucible which may yet boil them to the surface and to integrity.

### Declining Age of Pubescence

Today's North American teens experience the onset of pubescence at about age twelve for girls and age thirteen for boys. Since these are mean ages, half of all girls and boys experience first menarche and first ejaculation before that age. Traced by medical records since 1840, the ages of the onset of pubescence have dropped dramatically.[2] Records of first menstruation indicate a mean of about seventeen and a half years for girls in 1840. There is no available data on first ejaculation, but it is safe to plot that age at just about a year older. When the intervening years are plotted by year and country, the Western European and United States lines descend parallel with each other; the U. S. A. data, which is available from 1900 forward, comes in younger and drops parallel with Norway and other countries.

Speculation about causes of earlier sexual/cognitive maturity has produced research questions which have led to documentation of these kinds of findings:

1. *Genetic enrichment.* If the parents originated in socially distant places, the children tend to mature more rapidly, to grow taller than their parents, and to reach sexual maturity earlier than their parents did.

2. *Climate.* Warmer climates and earlier maturity tend to go together.

**3.** *Diet.* Better nutrition, largely a matter of socioeconomic status of the family, tends to correlate with earlier sexual maturity and taller children. Some of our unusually tall young, however, are actually showing effects of technical malnutrition. The "junk food" addictions of our young tend to produce one side effect which interferes with the maturation of bones, especially the lower shank bone of the leg. When the "stop growth" signal from the ends of bones is interfered with, the growth continues for a longer period than normal. So diet has some deceptive effects, too.

**4.** *Social mixing.* Studies with cattle indicate that if females retained for breeding are exposed to a male before the females come into estrus or "heat," they will come into heat on an average of six months earlier and will enter first calving and lactation that much ahead of their dams. No similar observations are available for humans, but social exposure to early saturation with sexual stimulation is a likely source for earlier development.

**5.** *Light.* We have long known of the relationship between light and the reproductive activity of chickens. Lighted henhouses have increased egg production for decades. But the pineal gland, which is light sensitive in reptiles and certain mammals such as chickens, is, in humans, buried deep inside the brain. It has been thought until recently that it was without connections to light sources. What we now know is that an indirect network of channels sends light from the eye through a chiasmic connection down the spinal cord and up into the brain to the pineal gland. When any human experiences light, the pineal gland stops production of a chemical called melatonin. When melatonin is being released into the bloodstream, it neutralizes sexual production of the ovaries and the testes. In children, it stops the development of the entire sex system and slows down all related growth. With the increase of light in the world of our children we have evidently contributed to their earlier sexual maturity. And this speed-up evidently also surprises the "stop growth" mechanism in our bones, leading to increased height as the generations move along.[3]

We might think that our young would be helped by slowing down their sexual development. But arrival at adult form is such an important rite of passage in the inner world of the young woman or young man that any delay contrived by keeping them in the dark, would be likely to impair their sense of self-worth and to leave them at the mercy of adolescent seductions without the benefit of a fully ripening body and brain. Studies show that boys who mature slowly are under the most severe social disadvantage. Unless these late developing teens adapt socially to form friendships with younger teens who match their development, they are vulnerable to paying very high prices trying to prove their adulthood by going through the motions of behaviors not yet scrutinized by a myelinized brain.

Women are sometimes treated during menopause with a special schedule of light, even during sleep, to smooth out the final months of ovarian production. The Creator's magnificent lock-in between sexual maturity and the brain's capacity to do advanced moral reasoning is a further witness to how mysteriously and wonderfully we are made.

## The Phenomenon of Adolescence

For most of human history, the physiology of pubescence was matched by social rites of passage, and in a relatively short time a girl became a woman with full rights and privileges in the community. In a similar way, though typically with very different rites, the boy became a man.

Among the Dani Tribe in New Guinea, a modern day stone age people, the virginal girls wear leaf skirts. But their budding breasts are a public "thermometer" signaling the arrival at pubescence. When the signal appears, the girl will typically be "married" to an eligible male. She goes through "the winding on of skirts," the literal word for "marriage." This skirt, woven of tree roots, is wound between her knees and hipbones, below the groin. The matron's skirt inhibits her walking and is a lifelong reminder of her married state. She must repair and continue to wear that original skirt as long as she lives.

The Dani boys, in contrast, go naked until the enlargement of the genitals signals their maturity. Then a phallic stick is installed in a rite which denotes their "warrior" status. The penis is installed in a hollow gourd, with a loop around the scrotum. The tree-root string is then threaded up and out the end of the long carrotlike gourd, which may extend to three feet or more. There at the end the cord is tied. Then a second string around the waist secures the gourd in an upright position. The length or height of the gourd denotes tribal rank, with the chief's males wearing the longest phallic sticks. This stick constitutes the entire wardrobe of the typical male, except for his warrior ornamentation, which he dons for festive mock battles.[4]

In contrast to this "instant adulthood" based on pubescence, modern technological cultures like those in Western Europe and North America have developed a series of rites of passage which parcel out adult status over a longer period of time. Consider the conscious and spontaneous "rites" toward which we watch our young stretch:

1. Confirmation or Bar/Bas Mitzvah, typically at age twelve or thirteen.
2. Driver's license.
3. High school graduation.
4. Voting age of eighteen, and military registration.
5. "Legal age" of eighteen to twenty-one, sometimes with "drinking card."
6. College entrance and living away from home.
7. Marriage.
8. Economic independence.

"Adolescence" is a psychosocial phenomenon we have invented to serve as an umbrella over the ever longer span of years between childhood and full adult responsibility. Not every American child experiences all eight of the transitions above. But, until the young adult has taken responsibility for final moral choices and for persons other than the self, childhood continues.

Families are able to condense adolescence for their children by giving early responsibility and freedom, always accompanied by evaluation and reflection on the consequences of errors in judgment or of moral failure. Take a matter as simple as the child's use of money.

*Toward Freedom and Responsibility*[5]

When he was sixteen, our Mike enjoyed the management and use of a ten-year-old Chevy. "Six cylinders and a slush box," I heard him call it. In December, the ancient radiator hoses gave out, dumping the antifreeze and incurring a total bill of eighteen dollars before it was ready to roll again. Two weeks later, a heater hose of equal antiquity blew out and flushed another ten dollars' worth of coolant down the storm sewer.

Mike's friend Steve insisted on pitching in with the do-it-yourself replacement this time. In the process of helping, Steve put a metal screw through the heater core. Filled up and running, it lost another load of radiator coolant before they detected the small leak. The best deal on repairing the heater core ran up the bill another fifteen dollars. Naturally, there was another round of coolant. In two weeks' time, Mike laid out just under fifty dollars on the car, and he had the use of it only two days.

What should we, his parents, do? We discussed the options we saw:

1. Punish him for a series of bad judgments, ground him, and sell the car.
2. Go fifty-fifty with him on the bad luck and repairs.
3. Let him sweat through the bad experiences and dip into summer earnings to bail himself out.

We chose the third option, because we come from a long line of "early launchings." My parents were married at eighteen. I was nineteen and Robbie eighteen when we married. And our sons married at nineteen and twenty. We attached a "new car" to either of two goals achieved: college graduation or marriage, whichever came first. My parents had surprised us with a new Plymouth when we were married, even though they had not yet clearly established their own affluence. We switched to Chevrolet for our sons, but promised them a choice of a full-size family car of their selection. And we knew that if Mike were to be ready for adult responsibility, there was no time like the present antifreeze tragedy to let him bear the full brunt of his decisions and his luck. Life would present him with a whole string of similar disasters, we knew, except that never again would the total bill run below fifty dollars.

I am using the money factor from the adolescent-rites-of-passage list, because it so innocently illustrates how we might prepare our children for adulthood at a speed that would more nearly match their physiological and brain development. Let me extend the money discussion to set the tone for ushering the child into maturity in other areas as well:

1. *Be open about money.* Our most effective teaching on any subject is that which comes spontaneously in real life experience. Formal teaching sessions with our children tend to come off hollow. We sin against our children when we shield them from our own real dilemmas. The details of budgeting, tithing, investing, borrowing, and lending are so complicated as to defy simple descriptions, but the principles are simple enough to be grasped by any ten-year-old who is allowed to work through personal problems on the issues, guided by an interested parent. No amount of "teaching" about tithing or financial stewardship can offset the impact of what the child sees the parents actually doing about their own financial stewardship before God. Children can also learn confidentiality about "family business," especially if parents are always open with them, and if they stress the privacy of financial facts.

2. *Call family "huddles."* Let the whole family in on planning vacations, looking at money budgeted for the holiday, and deciding how to spend it: for camping gear to save motel costs, or for a shorter trip in more luxury, for example. Any change in the family's fortunes calls for family consultation: a raise, with additional resources to earmark for the future and cutbacks in family income equally illustrate the issues worth talking about.

3. *Clarify changing family priorities.* When should Dad quit his moonlighting? Maybe the children need to help make that recommendation, based on the economic impact of his being home more. Should Mom take a part-time job now that the youngest child is off to school? The teens will

have some perspective on that, since it means the loss of some comfort, some added responsibilities, and some additional family money. Parents of teens who are still addicted to driving the sports car of their Peter Pan phase are telegraphing faddishness to their emerging teens. A family-car-now choice, says, "We adapt to the immediate priorities." The children need all the help available to see how financial decisions reflect the real world of the family's resources.

4. *Let children handle some money.* As soon as children can recognize that coins are exchanged for goods, they need some money of their own to spend. All members of the family should have full control over some appropriate amount of the family's resources to spend as they choose. Younger children should receive their money in small coins, never bills or checks, to multiply the sense of ownership and pleasure. Children's money should be used for things they want now—not "saved for college." It is best if the children receive their money at home, not at the store. Since delay of gratification always helps to develop the capacity to wait, giving money at a time or place where it can be immediately spent misses the benefits of the delay, the fantasy, and the weighing of choices.

5. *Hand over some serious money.* A school-age child can predict the amount of money needed for a week. This figure, including some pleasure money and enough for a "tithe," becomes the base for a week's budget. I had put Mike through this strategy shortly before the age-sixteen anti-freeze fiasco. Then, I had asked, "Where shall we get the money you need?" I offered, "We have some family money to put into it, of course." In a flash, he said, "Well, I made two hundred dollars on Granddad Joy's farm last summer, and it's in the bank. I can put in some each week from there." He did, and what amazed me was that within six months, this thirst for autonomy had motivated him to earning money, and he proudly announced, "I won't be needing any more money each week. I can handle it myself." Almost without exception, your child will work for economic independence.

6. *Let mistakes happen.* If you step in to change your child's decision or to shield the child from the economic

consequences of a decision, you rob your child. It was all I could do to resist handing over fifty dollars to Mike to reimburse him for the antifreeze episode. But the crisp image of careful management would likely have been badly blurred, if not lost, and I might still be bailing him out. Today, not sixteen years later, Mike is an entrepreneur businessman, operating in four states, with two full-time employees. I find myself wanting *his* advice and respecting *his* judgment on a wide range of subjects, including financial matters.

If we are suffering from too many Fonzies and Peter Pans running loose in our society, and if Aldonza is the female counterpart with her instant-gratification behaviors, we will do well to condense adolescence through early transfer of freedom and responsibility.

## The Sexual Agenda

The sexual agenda runs well ahead of the money agenda for providing both moral content and motivation to pleasure. And the sexual agenda descends, like the sun and the rain, on the rich and the poor, the good and the evil. So, if we are searching for the single adolescent phenomenon most likely to win or lose the day for our young, it is likely their sexual energy. I wish here to discuss sexual potency or fertility, the sex systems and their vast differences, and how the combination of fertility and pleasure establish the crucible in which morality is uniquely put under the blowtorch of formation or destruction.

*Sexual potency and fertility.* Our sexuality is our single most important self-identity criterion. "It's a boy!" or "It's a girl!" was the first coherent statement uttered about each of us. And watch the emotional, self-esteem consequences of any sexually altering surgery even among the aging. Any sexual impairment strikes at the heart of our identity.

The adolescent has been presented a gift—confirmation that the sexual gift "works"—in the form of the menstrual cycle or ejaculation. Any medical or social intervention—such as easy birth-control devices or quick abortion—which tends to neutralize the mystery and power of sexual fertility, trivializes the core of the moral agenda. Among the early-active group of the sexually active adolescents, there is high resistance to the use of contraceptives, likely because they sense that they possess wonderful power in their fertility.

Some people speak of "sex drive" in discussing pubescence and adolescence. While there is a sense in which it is correct to speak of humans as having a sex drive, such descriptions are likely to miss the uniqueness of human sexuality. I much prefer to speak of humans as developing a sexual appetite. A sexual appetite may serve to "drive" a person toward intimacy, but it is more complicated than mere hormones, apparatus, estrus, and pleasure.

Both men and women experience their sexuality as a source of pleasure, quite beyond the mere affirmation of sexual identity and self esteem. Sexual arousal occurs in both sexes, repeatedly, and several times a day, beginning with the onset of pubescence. The arousal is rooted in the hormonal saturation of pubescence and of adult mature sexuality. Sexual response in the context of relationships seems to be intrinsic to females but learned by males. But this differentiation opens the door on the second major facet of the adolescent sexual agenda:

*The sex systems.* The male system, as you recall from an earlier chapter, is formed out of the basic female embryo. Since it is the "inverse" of the female system, there are major similarities, but there are also striking differences.

Think of the female as having a "process system."[6] By this, I mean that the reproductive activity is controlled by an internal clock: the production of the monthly ovum, the storage of nutrients to undergird conception and fetal development, then the expulsion of these unused nutrients during the menstrual period. All of this process moves along with regularity in an adult female, without direct stimulation of pleasure. Some women report increased sexual awareness, susceptibility to arousal, and an estrus-like motivation toward a male. But this, too, is in a cyclical pattern which is keyed to the reproductive processes. Women, like men, experience sexual arousal during sleep—quite unrelated to the content of dreams but in a cycle matching the dream cycle as observed by noting the rapid-eye-movement phenomenon. These occur at ninety-minute intervals during postpubescent sleep.

Males, in contrast, might be described as having a "hydraulic system," a terminology to which I was first introduced by Dr. Boyd McCandless. By "hydraulic," I mean that the seminal fluids engorge the prostate glands, heightening the susceptibility to sexual arousal. The buildup of fluids is then expelled under pressure of sexual stimulation, arousal, and manipulation. In such a system, the pleasure is intrinsically linked to the reproductive system. Theoretically, a woman might live out a normal lifetime, bear children, but never experience clitoral stimulation and orgasmic climax. But every normal male will experience arousal and climax at every ejaculation. Looked at from the other side, a male may experience sexual climax only when going through the motions of reproductive activity. His capacity for sexual pleasure is limited to his reproductive system. A female, however, is capable of experiencing almost unlimited numbers of climaxes in a very short time span, since physiological reproduction resources are not linked to the genital activity.

So, among young children, girls are as likely as boys to discover sexual pleasure and embarrass the family by genital manipulation. Girls are even more likely, it would appear, to develop a sexual appetite for pleasure through early manipulation. But young men at pubescence experience a transformation of physiology which "charges" their hydraulic system and introduces them, even against their will, to sexual pleasure. The pleasure is so intrinsically locked in to reproduction, that they tend to become much more heavily involved in masturbation as adolescents than do young women. Typical studies consistently show that males masturbate an average of four times per week following pubescence, whereas among females who masturbate (and many do not) the average frequency is twice a month or once each two weeks. Typically, mothers who discover that their sons are masturbating lack a perspective with which to contemplate what is happening.

Just as a woman's menstrual cycle is predictable and healthy, so also a man's ejaculation frequency becomes predictable and important to his sense of well-being. The largest study of sexual behavior reported that a male's sexual appetite is formed by the end of thirty-six months after his first ejaculation. This appetite tends to hold during the age-twenty-through-age-fifty decades, showing a mild decline, but never an end, across the closing decades of life. The frequencies of ejaculation ranged, in the population sample of 12,000 males, from .5 to 21 times per week.

The female "process system" tends also to support the woman's sense of wholeness about sexuality. She tends to see her femaleness as projected toward relationships and an ultimate intimacy in which she possesses a man who participates in her entire life.

The male "hydraulic system" tends to call attention to the genitals and their pleasure. Whereas the woman experiences her sexuality as a psychosocial experience, the male is triggered by a biological-psychological-social combination. The male's first sexual pleasure tends not to be relational, but is almost purely a raw biological pleasure. The task of becoming truly human, for the male, requires that the raw pleasure be converted into fuel for establishing and cultivating a significant relationship. Males, typically Fonzies and Peter Pans, who do not move from the raw pleasure of their sexuality into the painstaking work of establishing a significant, exclusive relationship tend still to use the raw sexually aggressive gestures and verbal symbols of early adolescence. The four-letter-words and the finger gestures that once denoted sexual activity then become, by age twenty-five, words of mere raw aggression, meaning—in rough translation—"I'll bust your face!"

Given the very diverse intrinsic differences in the sex systems of males and females, it is easy to spot their uniqueness. We see the differentiated sexuality in the typical well-formed bride and her groom. Ask her about the wedding and coming marriage. She typically has a

GLOBAL, SUBJECTIVE, RELATIONAL PERSPECTIVE

on the whole matter. She is eager to talk with you about where "we" will live, what "we" will be doing, the apartment, the pattern for silver, china, and crystal. She is booked for showers, teas, and rehearsals, and everything is converging on a thirty-minute ritual which will tie all of these many parts into a gorgeous, bounteous bow: the bond of matrimony.

Ask a groom about the wedding. You are likely to find that he is interested in only one thing: the wedding night. He has a

CONCRETE, OBJECTIVE, PHYSICAL PERSPECTIVE

on the marriage. He may not admit how preoccupied he is with the genital consummation he sees ahead. But he is enduring tuxedos, shopping tours, selection of patterns for silver, crystal, and china. He will show up for the rehearsal, and he will host the dinner which follows. But he shows genuine excitement when he is reserving the hotel, planning the wedding trip. All of the price seems to be worth it when he considers that he will be joined physically with the one exclusive woman of his life.

What we now know is that the male's singular genital focus will tend, by mid-life, to have become diffused, until he is more global and relational in his priorities. He needs the cradling hold of his wife, just as she wanted to be held, not always involved sexually, on their honeymoon. And, by mid-life, under his expert genital tutoring, she is more likely to be sexually aggressive. Her sexual appetite has been given its shape over two or more decades of following his agenda. Now that his hormonal batteries are fading, she is able to focus his sexual energy into genital contact at a time when he may be fearing that his once mighty prowess is gone.

What we have watched from fetal development has now expressed itself in the highly differentiated sexuality of adolescence. From this point on, the movement toward each other will see the two sides of the image-of-God/male-and-female forming each other into highly similar mirrors of each other.

*The crucible.* Combine the deeply rooted, identity-bestowing sexual physiology with the pleasure and motivation to relationship which comes with the sexual awakening, and you have the ingredients for a profoundly personal, deeply sexual life crucible which is almost the pure essence of the moral and the spiritual.

It is spiritual in the sense that sexual attraction and the ultimate sexual intimacy are metaphors of the human union with God. And the gestures of eros, since they are human expressions of worship and adoration, are always echoing toward the Creator as vibrations of celebration and thanksgiving, even when the actors are unaware of their Supreme Parent and Guarantor who stands just offstage. God is quite aware of them and grants them the unconditional gifts even when they are quite unaware of their Source.

So, during the adolescent crucible when the freedom and responsibility are being hammered by social experience, it is the pain which will be the catalyst for producing either saints or monsters. I suspect, but cannot know, that one may suffer almost equally from trying to protect virginity and to abstain from inappropriate intimacy as from loss of virginity and dealing with the consequences of inappropriate intimacy. We would always choose innocence for ourselves and our young, but in my experience I have seen people who have failed to mellow out of virginity and others who are still trapped in their sexual tragedies.

On the other hand, I have seen both virgins who were not proud and formerly active and irresponsible people who are now mellowed and redeemed. *I conclude that it is how one deals with life experience, especially pain, not the experience itself that forms character.* Hence, I suggest that the adolescent crucible is an essential life passage for bringing persons to significant moral and spiritual maturity.

## Jesus and Pubescence

I once wrote a chapter for a book on youth ministry. I was to deal with "adolescence in psycho-social perspective." My opening line ran: "Jesus was once a teenager, but he was never an adolescent." The editors struck that line, to my chagrin. I wanted to define adolescence, as I have done in this chapter, from a cultural perspective. But there is a sense in which I was indeed wrong. Jesus, in his life of celibacy, lived out his entire post pubertal life in the crucible of what we now call "adolescence." It may be that our efforts to understand *singleness* and its relationship to *celibacy* will fail miserably unless we deal with the issues of fertility and pleasure and their obligation to integrity. Hence, celibacy is the form that Christian singleness takes. And, in celibacy, one sacrifices sexual energy and appetite on the altar of service to God.

And on a closer reading of the Gospels, I conclude that we have a fairly typical record of Jesus' entry into pubescence. It is in the account of Jesus' first visit to the Jerusalem Temple:[7]

> Every year his parents went to Jerusalem for the Feast of the Passover. When he was twelve years old, they went up to the Feast, according to the custom. After the Feast was over, while his parents were returning home, the boy Jesus stayed behind in Jerusalem, but they were unaware of it. Thinking he was in their company, they traveled on for a day. Then they began looking for him among their relatives and friends. . . .
>
> Luke 2:41–44

So what's new? Boy reaches pubescence, and you can't keep track of him. Where is he? You think you know, so you don't worry. Well, you'd better worry. If anything can go wrong, it will!

> When they did not find him, they went back to Jerusalem to look for him. After three days they found him in the temple courts, sitting among the teachers, listening to them and asking them questions. Everyone who heard him was amazed at his understanding and his answers. . . .
>
> Luke 2:45–47

Three days! What would you do if you knew your child were missing in a major city for three days? Go crazy, that's what. But notice that his adultlike thinking is evoking the respect of the teachers in the temple. Reflective, evaluative thinking has evidently shown itself here at the rite-of-passage event which sees Jesus first at the Temple.

> When his parents saw him, they were astonished. His mother said to him, "Son, why have you treated us like this? Your father and I have been anxiously searching for you."
>
> Luke 2:48

Here is the understatement of the first century! The boy is lucky it was not Joseph who spoke. But even the restraint of the mother is stated in "egocentric" terms: "Why have you treated us like this?" It was not even the "heterocentric" concern, "We have been worried about your safety." Here is the comfort we need as we face the life-threatening span of years known as our children's pubescence and adolescence.

> "Why were you searching for me?" he asked. "Didn't you know I had to be in my Father's house?"
>
> Luke 2:49

Look at this healthy son. Egocentrism again: "I knew where I was, why were you worried?" Friends of ours in Turfland Mall one afternoon heard a four-year-old racing down the mall yelling, "That does it! That does it! Now Mommie and Aunt Ethel are both lost!" Jesus was not lost. He was following his destiny and they could trust him. There is clearly a high level of mutual respect in this family transaction.

> But they did not understand what he was saying to them.
>
> Luke 2:50

Where there is respect, it is acceptable to allow some things to go without full mutual understanding. And teens need reassurance that their parents may not always understand them, either. It happened with Jesus and his parents.

> Then he went down to Nazareth with them and was obedient to them. But his mother treasured all these things in her heart. And Jesus grew in wisdom and stature, and in favor with God and men.
>
> Luke 2:51–52

The issue cuts both ways. There may be gaps in understanding, but the pubescent son continues in his pattern of obedience. He is obedient to parents who "do not understand." And in the adolescent crucible that delivered Jesus a fully formed male, the fully delivered Son of God, he is reported growing in wisdom and stature, and in favor with God and with the people. How could the description of the outcome of the adolescent crucible end on a higher note? Truly, there is life after puberty.

QUESTIONS PEOPLE ASK

*Q: I'm baffled by my son's masturbation. I know he does it, and my husband simply refuses to confront him about it. What should I do? He's very secretive about it, but still I know he does it.*

A: If your husband won't confront the masturbation issue, it is probably because he is still baffled by his own sexuality, and he is refusing to lie to his son. Mothers rarely understand the male system. Remember that the sexual appetite is formed during the thirty-six-month period following first ejaculation. If a young man does not begin masturbation or intercourse, his spontaneous "wet dream" evacuation will occur. With deep-sleeping boys, they sometimes are quite unaware of the sexual pleasure of those ejaculations. But most boys discover the pleasure and do manually manipulate to ejaculation. The most conscientious young men will avoid intercourse, regarding it as a moral taboo—fornication. Yet, such scrupulous youngsters may try so hard for "control" that they tend to increase their preoccupation with masturbation. Many of them suffer deep feelings of shame and humiliation. Some sense that they are out of control. It is these most frustrated boys who will develop the highest output appetites. They will be masturbating at night, in the shower, in the morning, and on and on.

In contrast, the boys who begin intercourse early will be characterized by the lowest masturbation frequencies of all, since they will consistently wait until they are able to arrange the social circumstances to have the privacy for sexual intimacy.

There are some guidelines that may help:

• There is no explicit mention of masturbation in the Bible, and there are no implied taboos. The "Onan" citation is patently false, since Onan's sin consisted of failing to impregnate his brother's widow to raise up a son to own the family inheritance.[8] But that is a difficult point to make in today's culture. With today's long delay after pubescence, it is virtually inevitable that males will either masturbate or make their way into social sexual intimacy.

• What your son does with his sexual energy is his contract with the Creator. You might help him to appreciate the fine sexual energy he has been given. He should know that his sexual appetite is his very own, that no one else may be quite like him, but that he is well within the boundaries of normal. Suggest that he consecrate his sexual energy to God, ask God to help him keep a pure mind, and focus on the marriage and intimacy that is waiting for him. I said to my son, after explaining the male sex system, "I will not be prying into your behavior. What you do with it is your responsibility. I know you will let God help keep you pure and innocent for your wedding day."

• Watch for signs of preoccupation with masturbation. These may include (1) avoiding social activities, preferring to be alone at home; (2) lack of social poise and ease with young women; (3) heavy looks of the "weight of the world" on his shoulders. All of these tend to occur when he feels trapped in a sea of shame. You can lift the shame by helping him to understand his amazing sex system.

*Q: You have not really said whether masturbation is right or wrong. Which is it?*

A: To say it is virtually "inevitable" is not to say it is right. But it is clear that young males are placed in a much more likely position to begin masturbating at pubescence than are young females.

I would stress that feelings of shame are inappropriate at any age. If I found a preschool child at self manipulation or engaged in exploratory mutual sex play, I would try to avoid traumatizing the event by the use of punishment or discipline. The curiosity is healthy and the body's responses are God's gift. Offer the children a tea party or other distractions, and ask your child not to put her hand in her diaper when there are guests in the house. Parental overreaction almost surely locks the child into continuing the behavior for a longer time than low-key diversion.

While the frequency of climax by masturbation is pale among females as compared to males, masturbation is common among young girls and female adults. Women who have never in their lives masturbated tend to show up as a group in that portion of the marital population which is nonorgasmic in intercourse. For many, it simply requires several months or even years of developing sexual appetite that responds to the husband's affection. Oldest daughters who were the family's "good girl" model tend to show up in this nonmasturbating, low-orgasmic-response group more often than any other family placement or type of woman.

Adolescent masturbation brings inevitable, though typically mild, guilt. I suspect this is because every adolescent brain is able to reflect: "I know I was made for something better than this. The feelings are good, but it is not good to be alone." Therefore, the most spiritually minded, chaste person has a yearning for an ultimate, permanent, intimate relationship. This intrinsic longing will evoke feelings of sadness which are a mild form of legitimate guilt. I use the word *guilt* here, as always, to denote some failure in a social setting where another person might hold a grievance, and where restitution is demanded and confession is a prerequisite to healing and forgiveness.

Masturbation within marriage amounts to the waste of intimate resources which belong to the maintenance of the Creation bond. Honesty about the level of one's sexual appetite is essential in every marriage and from both partners. "I told my wife I had never masturbated before we were married, but I lied," one of my fine students told me. "Now, I discover that I would have been pretty low on sexual motivation if I hadn't stumbled into it. I wish I had told her the truth." I affirmed him and indicated that he would tell her some day. "But you don't know my wife," he said, "she couldn't handle that kind of information."

"Don't underestimate the strength of a good woman," I said. Then I probed, "Are you masturbating now, in your marriage?"

"I can't believe you asked me that," he winced, slouching in the chair.

"You will want to tell her that, too." I said. "It all belongs to her, like 'money in the bank,' and she deserves to know what is available in terms of your healthy appetite."

"I know she couldn't handle that!"

Before he left my office he had courageously and spontaneously said, "I'm going to tell her tonight."

"You don't have to hurry. Any time in the next few years is okay, but it's definitely on your agenda. If anything 'hits the fan' here's my phone number. Robbie and I are at home tonight, and we have worked through it, so give us a call if you need us."

But we did not hear from him that night. The next morning my young friend was walking in circles in front of my office door, all smiles.

"You won't believe what happened!"

"Try me. I'll believe it."

"Well, I waited, like you told me, until I had her in my arms, then I told her the whole truth. She broke down and began to cry. I thought, *You dummy! You blew it!* But she soon got her voice and said, 'Honey, if you would tell me all of that, I know you will tell me anything. I will always trust you."

Now, ten years later, that pastor tells me to spread the word. The sexual appetites of two partners can be adjusted to match the maximum output of a very high frequency husband, if he will become not only an expert lover but an honest man.

When a conservative author absolutely forbids masturbation as demonic, I am troubled with the efforts at biblical distortions, and I suspect a bit of unreality in the writer's views about the Creation and human sexuality. On the other hand, when a more liberal author takes the position that masturbation is an unqualified good thing, I sense that this author has not grappled with the relational nature of human sexuality. And when still another prominent speaker says, "It's okay if you don't fantasize," I respond that if such were possible it would be very dangerous. Sexual arousal begins in the brain where a chemical is triggered and dropped into the bloodstream. That chemical blocks the blood's flowing away from the genital area. This fills the genitals with blood and causes the erection in the male, and the enlarging clitoris and vaginal canal in the female. Only brain stimulation will cause such an arousal. Random and unmotivated arousals, then, would be highly abnormal and robotlike mechanical episodes.

So, my position is that your sexuality is a gift from God, and your sexual energy and sexual appetite are unique to you. You are the sole steward of that marvelous gift. You must not violate other people or allow them to violate you. Your genitals are your own "private zone," and only your husband or wife should ever enjoy them with you. Tell anybody else, "No!" and "Never."

*Q: I have heard of nocturnal emissions or wet dreams, but what is this about "ninety-minute intervals"?*
**A:** The best and newest research on rapid eye movement and dreaming shows that under electronically monitored and filmed study of adults during sleep, sexual arousal occurs in ninety-minute intervals in both males and females.[9] Sexual arousal in a female is less often detected by the woman herself, as many studies have shown, but when measured by electrodes attached to the genitals, it can be verified electronically. Males often awaken in the night with full erections, even those who never in their lives have had a wet dream. My father told me the best he knew when he sent me to the bathroom as a young teenager and told me it was a sign I needed to urinate. But those nighttime erections are produced either by the deep, unconscious brain, or by the nonverbal hemisphere. Although they occur simultaneously with the ninety-minute dream cycles which are essential for health maintenance, they are, perhaps surprisingly, not typically accompanied by sexually related dream content. They usually last up to about thirty minutes, often undetected. If such an arousal is used as a basis for attempted intercourse, it often seems to have an artificial character. While males can maintain such an erection, it is not connected to the same climax system to which they are accustomed. Such experiences tend to underscore the

uniquely human necessity of establishing and cultivating a relationship for the human sex systems to reach their highest purposes.

*Q: If brain activity is essential to sexual arousal, what do I say to young people about fantasy? Isn't sexual fantasy "lust," and under the judgment of God?*

A: The New Testament word which gets translated "lust"—as, for example, in Jesus' words in Matthew 5:27–30—is not based on our word for pornography. That word becomes "fornication" and means, as I have explained elsewhere, "sex for sex's sake." But Jesus uses a much stronger word, built on a Greek stem which implies the hypnotic pursuit of a sexual object as if one were "in heat." Thus, the apostle Paul can caution us to "flee youthful lusts" and can take in all of those objects for which anyone would risk life and limb to get. Think of animals in heat. Nothing can stop them short of violent interference. Jesus is saying that this solid internal decision to have that person's body for oneself is under the judgment of God. And we know that both mental and literal fornication are also under the judgment of God. But that still leaves us with positive, sanctified images of sexual intimacy, and youthful fantasy easily focuses on future consummation of marital dreams. When one of our sons stashed away some *Playboy* centerfolds which showed up in the weekly housecleaning, I returned them to him.

"I'm glad to know that you are interested in girls," I said.

He gulped and said nothing.

"As a Christian, you may want to be careful not to get hooked on 'sex on paper,' " I said, "because Christians know that the real thing is much more interesting. And it would be a pity on your wedding night to fall into the arms of your wife and have to conjure up the memory of some *Playboy* picture to keep a good erection. Some of your friends are going to get hooked on sex movies and magazine pictures. And they will not be as warmly intimate in their marriages. In fact, 'sex on paper' and 'sex in the movies' is really anti-sex, because it keeps you from developing respect-based relationships with real people."

I had his full attention, but he was not responding. So I went on: "When you need to think about the wonderful thing God has done by creating you male and by creating half of the race female, I recommend that you think of specific young women you know and respect." I named a half dozen with whom I knew him to be quite close, in a ninth-grade social set which group-dated several times each month. "If you think of how God is going to give you someone as pure and gracious as any one of them is, I won't worry about your ever doing anything sexually that would hurt or damage her or you. But if you get hooked on 'sex on paper' or 'sex in the movies,' it is anybody's guess what you might do 'just for kicks.' "

# 9

# Life, Love, and Eternity: The Ultimate Intimacy

△

I first saw Stan at the dinner table in his parents' parsonage home when I was the guest preacher. I saw him now and then across the next ten years. At last, I learned that he had gone away to university and experienced the high-risk adolescent rebellion of the sixties. He slipped into the drug culture with its loose sex. During that lost period, I was given one night with him. He lay there in the near dawn silence of our room in another parsonage where a mutual friend had arranged for a rendezvous. When, near morning, I turned over to sleep, I said, "Stan, I'm glad for this time with you, but I expect we are saying 'Good-bye' with this chance meeting. We have chosen very different life targets, and our paths aren't likely to cross again."

I went on: "I hope that you find the dreams you are pursuing. I'm afraid you have chosen paths that are completely unfamiliar to me. And around some corner, somewhere, someday, I hope I will see you again." We relaxed and slept.

Ten years later, a week after Easter, a letter came from Stan. It told how "sin has blocked our communication for all of these years." He had "come home" to family and to faith. But it was the instrument of his return that stunned me. I now have another ten years of reflection on the story, and I also have Stan's permission to tell it here.

During his drug and sexual misadventures, Stan met Della. They took off together, traveled internationally, even finished some graduate-school work. Then, overseas, the money ran out; the drug bonanza became too risky. A collect call home to a brother got two airline tickets into the computer, and they flew home from a distant capital. Within the week, on Easter morning, Stan melted at the kitchen table in his parents' home, and like the prodigal, was repentant—which means, ultimately, "to come home to the truth."

Stan told me later how the mellowing, the reflection, and the repentance were triggered: "Della, a frightened woman from a troubled home, showed me how much she really trusted me and loved me. Whenever I held her in my arms and looked into her eyes, I was stabbed with a sweet yearning mixed with the guilt of my running away from the God who had created all of this. It was the way she looked into my eyes that let me know, six thousand miles from home, that I was coming home to God."

## Intimacy: God's Curriculum for Eternity

Dennis Kinlaw, distinguished scholar and preacher, and my warm personal friend, has traced the work of Charles Williams and others in distinguishing among literalism, symbol, allegory, image, and experience.[1] In summary:

*Literalism* limits the power of a story or an event to the surface facts and realities. It allows for no meaning beyond itself.

*Symbol,* as defined by Samuel Coleridge, (a) exists in itself, but (b) derives from something greater than itself, and (c) must represent in itself that greatness from which it derives.

*Allegory* is an artistic construction, one kind of symbol, which is crafted specifically to convey a message. When we speak of "metaphor," we commonly are crafting analogies between the known and the less well known; we make one category illustrate another.

*Image* exists in its own right, with no trace of any artificial or mechanical "message," and remains to be discovered "as part of the viewer's world." Unlike the allegory which is a deliberate deductive tool, the image awaits inductive discovery. The most powerful symbols, then, are images, since they break over us suddenly, even before we can prepare our defenses, as in the case of Stan's looking into Della's face.

*Experience* is our day-to-day contact with reality. It is experience that furnishes our own personal "private curriculum" of life. Much of it appears to be mere experience, but to those who think about what is happening there appear patterns or images which give a sort of third dimension. Then, these main lines in the mural of our lives may begin to take on "meaning" and eternal significance. God is speaking in "images."

Dr. Kinlaw arranges the Williams-Coleridge literary foundation to form a base from which he approaches the Song of Solomon. Of "Song of Songs," Kinlaw says,

> . . . there is not a suggestion in the text of the wide variety of spiritual insights that the commentators of all types have drawn from this little volume through the centuries. One hardly gets the feeling that the original participants in this drama of human love had in the forefront of their consciousness all of the exalted themes which commentators find so evident.[2]

And precisely here, Kinlaw draws on Williams and Coleridge and their distinctions about symbols as image:

> . . . faithful married love . . . has its own existence. It is good in itself. It does not need to be spiritualized to have human worth. It should be enjoyed for what it is in itself. Yet it can not but speak of more. . . .
>
> Human love is thus not first a human experience that helps us understand God. It is a personal experience that helps us relate joyously to one another. . . . But it is not an earthly category that just happens to illustrate a divine reality. It is a human experience that images something eternal. It is part of what Scripture means by the *imago Dei*.[3]

In this chapter I want to round out the thesis of the whole book: *Basic human intimacies are images of the most pro-*

*found spiritual reality;* they are God's "first curriculum." They are available equally to rich and poor—the best things in life *are* free! Not everyone sees the images, but for those who do, human existence and eternal reality are united into glorious stereophonic beauty.

Then, I want to retrace the human development pathway to show how it unfolds in a repeating pattern with ever-enlarging images. With each expansion and its repetition, we are nearer "the thing of which the image is only a representation." And that thing is the eternal reality: life unending in joyous community with God and with others.

## Attachment: "Hold Me Tight!"

Watch the bonding peaks in human life. Here, and in the following sections, look at them first in three slices from the life cycle:[4]

| INFANCY | ADULTHOOD | LIFE'S END |
|---|---|---|
| Birth Bonding | Pair Bonding | In the arms of God |

Created as we were from the hand of God and walking daily in the "cool of the day" in intimate conversation and joyous companionship with God, the birth bonding of the human race was to its original Parent. That intimacy, experienced as we now do with our natural parents in the first hours of life, is evidently the foundation image and practice arena for future intimacy with spouse, and ultimately with God.

Recent research reports show that adolescent children are, in the eighties, more attached to their parents than previous research probes have found. They trust their parents, consult them for advice, and regard them as their friends. This trend, now twenty years away from the sixties, may be rooted in the sensitized parent behaviors that saw them enter the world into the arms of fathers as well as of mothers, and also saw the elimination of radical anesthesia during normal delivery. Again, it is clear that this set of images hangs together, and may bring us even to our deaths with a sense of attachment to the eternal Parent and the eternal community.

"Hold me tight!" is the persistent human cry, but it is always gesturing toward God the Parent, toward God the Lover, and finally toward God who walks with us through "the valley of the shadow of death."

### Faithfulness: "Never Let Me Go!"

A sense of dependency responds to the guarding, protecting parent. Watch the flow:

| INFANCY | ADULTHOOD | LIFE'S END |
|---------|-----------|------------|
| Hold me! | Embrace me! | Let me hold on! |

We watch the clinging behavior of young children. And we smile at the "clutching" of young lovers as they huddle together in the front seat of the car or walk down our streets. Finally, we stand with our dying parent or child and feel the eager pull as, between two worlds, they gesture for us to ease the crossing by holding tight. But we release them into the safe grip of God's hand for eternity.

On the other hand, there is a larger appeal in our cry. It has a cosmic dimension. "Never let me go!" also signals our need for the fidelity/faithfulness of uninterrupted care:

| INFANCY | ADULTHOOD | LIFE'S END |
|---------|-----------|------------|
| Don't abandon me! | Live in faithfulness! | Into your hands. . . . |

There it stands. The lifelong string of images of interpersonal faithfulness. With the infant, "out of sight" means abandonment. But by adolescence the universal dream is for one person who will remain faithful unto death, even though devastated by economic or physical tragedy. Present or absent, the spouse is envisioned as always faithful and exclusive in the covenant forged between them. Then, facing death, even though the intermittent cry is "Don't forsake me, God!" the final peaceful breath is "into your hands I commit my spirit."

God enters into a covenant with Israel. Abraham finds God standing by as a nourisher or suckler through all of life's adventures of obedience. God's faithfulness holds even when Israel is a harlot and lives in infidelity to the heavenly Husband. And Job is able to cry out against all adversity and against all of his theological questions which remain unanswered: "Though God slay me, yet will I trust God" (see Job 13:15).

### Freedom: "Give Me Space!"

Is intimacy the enemy of autonomy? Or is it the essential alternate heartbeat? Watch the paradox as freedom protects from adversary-like "distantiation":

| INFANCY | ADULTHOOD | LIFE'S END |
|---|---|---|
| "I can do it myself!" | "Owning my own life and vocation!" | "Going to my own place!" |

Parents rejoice to see the day when the child can handle the toilet detail "all by myself." They wave good-bye to son or daughter off for college and off into marriage and new covenant relationships. And there is a fitting sense of crossing the river, alone, to find the personal space among the "many rooms" which the Groom has gone ahead to prepare for all of us who follow.

In *Secrets*, his little book for parents, Paul Tournier puts forward a remarkable thesis about children's need for privacy.[5] The main lines are simple, and easy to observe:

1. Young children need privacy. A private drawer or a locked box to which only they have the key will do. The children's privacy establishes a space in which they can construct their individuality. Children denied privacy tend to have trouble with issues of identity. They may lie—to create an inner private space to which intruding adults have no access. Or they may become violent, determined to find space through creating distance.

2. Emerging adolescents, as adults, need to share their secrets. They will handpick their confidential friend or

friends. They "unpack" the locked box and disclose their inner secrets. They tend to say, "I've never told anyone this before. . . ." Only in sharing the secrets does the individual embrace personhood.

3. Finally, the ultimate possession of personhood is seen in repentance and faith as we "tell all of our secrets to God" and commit to God even those things about ourselves which we do not quite understand.

Parents, then, who deny the child privacy and his or her own secrets tend to deny the child access to individuality. Then, when the body ripens and the surge to leave is strong, the adolescent may have very few secrets to present in the intimate setting where attaining personhood needs to occur.

When I once shared the Tournier formula for bringing our children to personhood and maturity, a venerable minister volunteered this story:

His son Mark, at thirteen, was in his room with the door closed and locked. He had just arrived home from school. His mother, seeing the closed door, called to him.

"I'm busy."

"What are you doing?"

"I'm just busy, that's all!"

"Can I come in?"

"No, not now!"

She tried the doorknob and, finding it locked, reached to the top of the bathroom door facing for the passkey to the universal locks in the house. Inserting it quietly, she opened the door.

Mark fell over some papers on his desk, cramming one handful into the drawer and "locking" the desk top itself with his body. He grasped the back of the desk and lay face down covering the work.

His mother began pulling at him, finally yanking over the chair. Mark and the desk fell into the center of the room. By now Mark was angry and was sobbing violently. He stormed out of the room and locked himself in the bathroom.

On the floor now and crammed into the top drawer of

the desk were the remains of an originally designed and crafted Mother's Day greeting!

The now-sensitive, ready-to-retire minister said wistfully, "It took more than ten years for Mark to heal from that five-minute episode, and I'm not sure, of course, that he or his mother will ever know what was lost then."

God has created the first humans and us for freedom, and he has left us to make creative decisions independently. Our identity is both as "God's children" and as "ourselves," distinct from God. We may choose to rebel, even to commit treason against God, and thus to indulge in deliberate "distantiation" of a tragic and destructive sort. But the freedom which embraces responsibility is essential to our true reflection of God's own nature. To be "in relationship" does not suggest a parasitic, neurotic inability to soar alone as sons and daughters of the Creator.

We experience God as Liberator, as cheering Audience, as applauding Spectator. God presents the gifts and yearns to see us use them. God grants the resources and rejoices to see us exercise creative management.

## Risk: "Jump Naked!"

Freedom and choosing evoke feelings of near fear. Remember the sensation in your abdomen when your parents drove over a quick rise in the road. Or think of your first roller coaster ride—or your last, for that matter. When we are quite sure that the wheels will engage on the other side, we rather like the sensation. We even pay money for the feelings. But something could go wrong. And it often does. Then the feelings are stark fear or terror.

Imagine what went through the minds of the passengers and crew aboard the giant airliner which dropped thirty thousand feet as a fuel tank went empty. Five thousand feet above the ground, the crew corrected a shut-off valve and opened a reserve tank, avoiding a crash. But if the Kentucky State Fair sold "rides" on a jetliner which was scheduled to make a thirty-thousand-foot drop, the same sensations would not be accompanied by the raw terror of that passenger load on the out-of-control airliner. Consider the risks by which we grow:

| INFANCY | ADULTHOOD | LIFE'S END |
|---|---|---|
| "Watch me jump! Did I do a history?" | "With all my earthly goods I thee endow!" | "To my children I bequeath. . . ." |
| Naked into the world | Naked and unashamed | Going out naked |

At Arlington, Texas, a church youth group was learning how to tell the truth, how to take Jesus seriously. Steve Moore, the youth minister, offered the analogy of how transparent Jesus calls us to be. We need to be able to own our problems, to confess our sins—"to jump naked." The image caught the imagination of the teens. I discovered the words written on the sealed side of an envelope delivered to my box when Steve was visiting. What might have been an obscenity, turned out to be a roller-coaster label denoting the exhilaration of "coming clean," of taking the risk of being a person of truth.

God is urging us to muster courage to leap for truth. God's own history of risk taking and truth telling acts like a magnet to pull us out the door to test our own parachutes. Who are you willing to have present when you come down to die? In the presence of the final weakness, who will be admitted through your door? What are your funeral plans? Can you write an epitaph with which you could live? Are there ideas or values for which you would be willing to die? On which hill are you prepared to dig in for some final defense? These are probes into your readiness to take the ultimate risk.

*Trust: "Knowing as We Are Known!"*

The final step in all intimacy is the test of full knowing. "Naked and unashamed" sets the stage, but "knowing" is the solid, continuing mutual respect of the finest bond. Look at the threefold cycle:

| INFANCY | ADULTHOOD | LIFE'S END |
|---|---|---|
| Delight to trust | No secrets hidden | Knowing as we are known |

Infants have no sense of shame. It arrives with self-consciousness and social teaching. Lovers begin slowly, but eventually open their entire hearts to each other. And eternity is the ultimate intimacy: a community, not just one-flesh pairs, that lives in absolute trust, transparency, and knowledge of one another.

## Images of the God-Human Intimacy

We have traced the image of God as Parent. The "double Adam" represents the full-spectrum God. But God's investment in the human creation attracts the "female" side of the imagery to the earthly presence. So God is Husband to Israel, God's Bride. Then Jesus arrives, the prototypic Bridegroom who leaves behind his other self: Christ the Bride. Faithfulness is the yearning of God for an ongoing relationship with Israel and the Bride. Atonement and grace set the stage for salvation, which images God's cleansing and covering the nakedness of the Bride. Finally, with the Marriage Supper of the Lamb, eternity ushers in the relationships for which we are always longing: we will know as we are known.

## Postscript: Who Loves Like God?

The images populate Scripture, but nowhere is the story told more explicitly and graphically than in Ezekiel 16:3–14.

This is what the Sovereign Lord says to Jerusalem: Your ancestry and birth were in the land of the Canaanites; your father was an Amorite and your mother a Hittite. On the day you were born your cord was not cut, nor were you washed with water to make you clean, nor were you rubbed with salt or wrapped in cloth. No one looked on you with pity or had compassion enough to do any of these things for you. Rather, you were thrown out into the open field, for on the day you were born you were despised.

Then I passed by and saw you kicking about in your blood, and as you lay there in your blood I said to you, "Live!" I made you grow like a plant of the field. You grew up and developed and became the most beautiful of jewels. Your breasts were formed and your hair grew, you who were naked and bare.

Later I passed by, and when I looked at you and saw that you were old enough for love, I spread the corner of my garment over you and covered your nakedness. I gave you my solemn oath and entered into a covenant with you, declares the Sovereign Lord, and you became mine.

I bathed you with water and washed the blood from you and put ointments on you. I clothed you with an embroidered dress and put leather sandals on you. I dressed you in fine linen and covered you with costly garments. I adorned you with jewelry: I put bracelets on your arms and a necklace around your neck, and I put a ring on your nose, earrings on your ears and a beautiful crown on your head. So you were adorned with gold and silver; your clothes were of fine linen and costly fabric and embroidered cloth. Your food was fine flour, honey and olive oil. You became very beautiful and rose to be a queen. And your fame spread among the nations on account of your beauty, because the splendor I had given you made your beauty perfect, declares the Sovereign Lord.

Move from Ezekiel's image to the culminating images of Revelation 21:1-2:

Then I saw a new heaven and a new earth, for the first heaven and the first earth had passed away, and there was no longer any sea. I saw the Holy City, the new Jerusalem, coming down out of heaven from God, prepared as a bride beautifully dressed for her husband.

Then follow, in chapter 22, the words of the Groom:

"I, Jesus, have sent my angel to give you this testimony for the churches. I am the Root and the Offspring of David, and the bright Morning Star."

The Spirit and the bride say, "Come!" And let him who hears say, "Come!" Whoever is thirsty, let him come; and whoever wishes, let him take the free gift of the water of life. . . .

The grace of the Lord Jesus be with God's people. Amen.
Revelation 22:16–17, 21a

In his book *The Great Divorce,* C. S. Lewis permits a busload of people from hell to visit heaven, with a view to their reconsidering past destructive choices with an option, yet, to take possession of eternity with God and holy community. Lewis portrays hell with an image of alienation and distantiation. In this book, I owe Lewis a great debt. For without that image of hell, it might not have occurred to me to regard "intimacy" as the ultimate human yearning and destiny.[5]

The fantasy journey begins on the streets of "that grey city" where it seemed always to be raining and enclosed in an evening twilight. Hell. Lewis casts the book in first person, as if the author himself were our window into the events. He is immediately cornered by a "Tousel-Headed Poet" who insists that he read a sheaf of poems.

The author objects to the Poet that "It seems a deuce of a town. . . . The parts of it that I saw were so empty. Was there once a much larger population?"

To this the Poet replies that the town is virtually empty. All one needs to do to create a new space is to "*think* a house and there it is." But the people are all so quarrelsome, and none trusts the other. Consequently, the population is daily shifting to find more space and to avoid contact with the other quarrelsome residents of the grey city.

The author asks about the first arrivals in hell. Where are they?

"They've been moving on and on. Getting further apart. They're so far off by now that they could never think of coming to the bus stop at all. Astronomical distances. . . . You can see the lights of the inhabited houses, where those old ones live, millions of miles away. Millions of miles from us and from one another. Every now and then they move further still. . . . a distance of light-years."

There it is. The human craving for intimacy and trust, when turned on its head, becomes a complete preoccupation with isolation and alienation. And heaven? The images of intimacy suggest that the entire population of the billions of the redeemed might be housed in a thimble, with plenty of space left over for privacy. To "know as we are known" suggests "naked and unashamed," once more—where private secrets become the pearls shared and enjoyed because the "swine" have disappeared and no longer threaten to trample our shared experience or rip us to shreds. Eternity—as ultimate trust and ultimate intimacy—is the driving image which unites these ideas.

I regret that C. S. Lewis left us without a glimpse of the Community of Trust and Love. But perhaps he is writing it, even now. Until we have the guidebook to the City, it is enough that we can contemplate the primer or the first curriculum: *Bonding: Relationships in the Image of God.*

# Notes

## 1. Who Is Holding Your Trampoline?

1. E. Mansell Pattison reports on his findings about the healthy "psychosocial kinship system" in his *Pastor and Parish—A Systems Approach* (Philadelphia: Fortress Press, 1977), pp. 18–19. I have greatly simplified the findings by suggesting the metaphor of a hand-held trampoline, and the interpretive and theological suggestions are my own.

2. I am indebted to Dr. Delbert Rose, my mentor in biblical studies during seminary days, for the perception that Hebrew and Eastern thought tends to move from the whole to the parts, from global to concrete, in contrast to Western thought. Dr. Rose first introduced me to the "internal structure" of 1 John 1 and its "global" organization.

Insights into East-West and right-left understandings of brain conceptions are emerging from everywhere.

The work of Roger Sperry on brain organization opened up the physiological implications from his study of surgically separated hemispheres in epileptic grand mal seizure patients. But Atuhiro Sibatani, in "The Japanese Brain: The Difference Between East and West May Be the Difference Between Left and Right," goes further and explains both language and culture in the "di-morphic" model (*Science/80*, December 1980), pp. 22 ff.

## 2. On Splitting the Adam!

1. I read secondary references to Karl Barth's notions about the "image of God." More recently, I have consulted the first four volumes of his *Dogmatics.* His support for what I am calling the "double image," male and female, is scattered through those early volumes and by no means organized into a coherent whole.

2. Edward L. Kessel makes the point about "reproduction without

187

gender" in his surprising article, "A Proposed Biological Interpretation of the Virgin Birth" (*Journal of the American Scientific Affiliation*, September 1983), pp. 129 ff. Here Kessel also cites much of the same sequence I report in chapter five on conception and fetal development.

3. Daniel Levinson, with others, released *The Seasons of a Man's Life* (New York: Ballantine Books, 1978).

4. When I suggest an intrinsic sex difference in the affective organization of life, I am following the validation data on the Myers-Briggs Personality Type Indicator which reports the only sex difference to be identified on the "thinking versus feeling" scale. And I am following the early reports on Carol Gilligan's research at Harvard. While these are early and small sample reports, Dr. Gilligan is in search of "a different voice" as the basis for moral reasoning in women. You can follow her work in "Woman's Place in Man's Life Cycle," in *Harvard Education Review*, volume 49, 1979, p. 444 ff.; and "A Naturalistic Study of Abortion Decisions," in Robert Selman and R. Yando, eds., *Clinical-Developmental Psychology* (San Francisco: Josey-Bass, Number 7, 1980), p. 70 ff.; and "In a Different Voice: Women's Conceptions of Self and Morality," in *Harvard Education Review*, No 47, 1977, pp. 492 ff. Finally, see also Gilligan's book: *In a Different Voice: Psychological Theory in Women's Development* (Cambridge: Harvard University Press, 1982).

5. Lawrence Kohlberg's research, along with Jean Piaget's, was almost exclusively done among males. Piaget's chapter three in *The Moral Judgment of the Child* (New York: The Free Press, 1965) is entitled "Cooperation and the Idea of Justice." That Piagetian discovery becomes the basis for "moral development research" in general, and Piaget's research was first published in French in 1932. Lawrence Kohlberg, in particular, has pursued the idea of justice as the "core of morality." See "The Primacy of Justice," a section of the larger chapter, "Stages of Moral Development as a Basis for Moral Education," in Clive Beck, et al., eds., *Moral Education* (Toronto: University of Toronto Press, 1970), pp. 62 ff. Kohlberg's most recent definitive work is *The Philosophy of Moral Development: Moral Stages and the Idea of Justice* (San Francisco: Harper and Row, 1981).

6. Harold Myra, *The Choice* (Wheaton: Tyndale House, 1980).

7. "Your desire shall be for your husband." It was Marie Powers of Seattle who, in her lectureship on "God's Purpose for Woman," first provoked me to look again at this assertion in the consequences of the woman's sin. Her sixth lecture, "The Desire of the Woman," elaborates her ideas on this text. A set of seven tapes is available directly from Mrs. Powers at 1823–207 Pl. SW, Lynnwood, Washington, phone (206) 778–7070.

8. Paul's idea of "headship" is treated today by highly competent biblical theologians. Fred Layman's "Male Headship in Paul's Thought," in *Wesleyan Theological Society Journal*, Volume 15, number 1, Spring, 1980, stopped me cold. Biblical theologians are our holy hope for setting the biblical text in its cultural context instead of own. Twentieth-century, North American ideas of "headship" evidently carry much baggage that

was not present in Paul's use of the term. An easily manageable and very popularly written article to the same point is the Berkeley and Alvera Mickelsen article, "The 'Head' of the Epistles," in *Christianity Today*, February 20, 1981, pp. 20 ff.

## 3. Pair Bonding: What God Joins Together

1. I will be citing and relying heavily on the work of Desmond Morris and Melvin Konner in chapters three and four. It is Morris' *Intimate Behavior* (New York: Random House, 1971) which details the twelve steps of pair bonding. I depart from his language on one of them as I reach for the most comprehensive descriptions for what he reports. Melvin Konner's *The Tangled Wing: Biological Constraints on the Human Spirit* (New York: Holt, Rinehart and Winston, 1982) carries significant discussion of pair bonding in animals and birds, issues which will be valuable to the next chapter.

2. Jesus on pair bonding is nowhere more explicit than in Matthew 19: "What God joins together, let not man put asunder." Jesus is quoting, of course, as does the apostle Paul more than once, from the doctrine of Creation and the classical pair-bonding statement of Genesis 2:24–25.

3. Desmond Morris, *Intimate Behavior*, p. 73.

4. My conversation with Dr. James Dobson about pair bonding was the substance of a taping session for his "Focus on the Family" radio show. That tape, Number 500, is available from Focus on the Family, Box 500, Arcadia, CA 91006. A series of six tapes is available with my best current articulation on pair bonding, from SPO 004, Wilmore, Kentucky 40390. Request pricing on "Basic Life Intimacy" tape set.

5. Desmond Morris, *Intimate Behavior*, pp. 101–102.

6. ". . . He can never divorce her as long as he lives" is the final word on the final case of sexual contact, reported in Deuteronomy 22:29.

7. See Alfred Kinsey, *Sexual Behavior in the Human Male*, (Philadelphia: W. B. Saunders Company, 1948), the chapter, "Religious Background and Sexual Outlet," pp. 465 ff.

8. I cite these titles to illustrate how deeply the "image" is stamped in the collective consciousness, yet neither author articulates the image-of-God/male-and-female quite like I am doing in this book. If the titles interest you, here are the full citations: Ruth Tiffany Barnhouse, *Homosexuality: A Symbolic Confusion* (New York: The Seabury Press, 1979), and Don Williams, *The Bond that Breaks: Will Homosexuality Split the Church?* (Los Angeles: BIM, Inc., 1978).

## 4. What Has Gone Wrong with the Bonding?

1. Jack Mabley reported in the *Chicago Tribune* (Wednesday, March 21, 1979, Section 1, p. 4) that *Playboy* had hoped to use the results of

a Lou Harris poll, which they had funded to bolster their theory that "a majority of men seek self-fulfillment and pleasure and approve of some drug use, cologne, mustaches, beards, bright clothes, and legalized gambling, marijuana, and prostitution." But Harris found quite another picture: "The singular mark of the American man, in terms of what he spends his leisure time on, is that he is something of a homebody, at best puttering around the house, not so much entertaining himself as being entertained or put to sleep by electronic or printed material produced by somebody else." After *Playboy* called a press conference to "use" its version of the Harris data, Harris himself called a conference to put out the full picture. It included: "Sixty-three percent said 'family life' was the most important thing in life. Fifty-four percent said a good sex life at home was essential in marriage, and 73 percent said the husband's fidelity was vital to a good marriage."

2. Tournament species in animals and birds are discussed in Melvin Konner's *The Tangled Wing*, cited in note 1, chapter three. See his chapter on "Lust," pp. 261 ff. His observation that humans fall into the "imperfectly bonding" category is from p. 273.

3. Find John Wesley's sermon "The General Deliverance" in any published set of his works. It falls just beyond the "standard fifty-two sermons" which tend to come first.

4. Elizabeth Kubler-Ross did the pioneer work on grief and reported it in her *Death and Dying* (New York: The Macmillan Company, 1969).

5. Zechariah, father of John the Baptist, hears the angel's prediction about his son who will come in the spirit and the power of Elijah. It is recorded in Luke 1:13–17.

## 5. Conception: Differentiating the 'Adam'

1. Follow the sexual differentiation in *The Body Human: The Sexes*, in the famous television or videotape series, to see and hear the amazing story of the transformation of the female system into the male. Read it, also, in M. J. Sherfey's *The Nature and Evolution of Female Sexuality*, (New York: Vintage, revised, 1972). See a newsmagazine story of the same thing in Pamela Weintraub's "The Brain: His and Hers," in *Discover*, April 1981, pp. 15 ff.

2. See Diane McGuinness, "How Schools Discriminate Against Boys," in *Human Nature*, February 1979, pp. 82–88.

3. Sexual orientation and its relation to brain development is addressed by Robert W. Goy and Bruce S. McEwen in *Sexual Differentiation of the Brain* (Cambridge: MIT Press, 1980), especially in the section "Is There an Endocrine Basis for Homosexuality Among Human Males?" pp. 64 ff.

4. The Dominican "Laboratory" is described in Julianne Imperato-McGinley's report, with others, "Androgens and the Evolution of Male-

Gender Identity Among Male Pseudohermaphrodites with 5a-Reductase Deficiency" in *The New England Journal of Medicine*, May 31, 1979, pp. 1233 ff.

5. Elizabeth Barrett Browning's lines are from *Aurora Leigh*, Book VII, lines 820 ff.

6. M. J. Sherfey, *The Nature and Evolution of Female Sexuality*, p. 48.

7. See both Alfred Kinsey's *Sexual Behavior in the Human Male* (1948 report on 12,000 interviews) and his *Sexual Behavior in the Human Female* (Philadelphia: W. B. Saunders Company, 1953, reporting on 8,000 interviews).

8. The now-famous *"Redbook* Report" based on the questionnaires of 100,000 women reported the "religious difference" under the flamboyant title "Why Religious Women Are Good Lovers," by Claire Safran, *Redbook*, April 1976, pp. 103 ff.

9. Carl Sagan has popularized the work of Nobel Prizewinner Roger Sperry of Cal Tech. Two marvelous chapters on the human brain appear in Sagan's *The Dragons of Eden* (New York: Random House, 1977).

10. On left-handedness and precision, see Sharon Begley's "Why Is Lefty So Different?" in *Newsweek*, August 20, 1982. Maya Pines', "The Sinister Hand," in *Science/80*, December 1980, pp. 26–27 is also astonishing.

11. G. L. Rico's *Writing the Natural Way* (Los Angeles: Tarcher Press, 1983).

12. A summary of the Geschwind and Behan studies is reported in Sharon Begley's article cited in Note 10 above.

13. Dan Kiley, *The Peter Pan Syndrome* (New York: Dodd and Mead, 1983).

14. See Kinsey, *Sexual Behavior in the Human Male*, "Homosexual Outlet," pp. 610 ff. A diagram of the seven gradients in sexual orientation of males appears on page 638. Type O is entirely heterosexual. Type 6 is entirely homosexual.

15. The Dorner study is reported in Robert Goy and Bruce McKewen, *Sexual Differentiation of the Brain*, pp. 64 ff.

16. See William Masters and Virginia Johnson, *Homosexuality in Perspective* (Little, Brown, Company, 1979). For referrals, the sex therapy clinic of William Masters and Virginia Johnson may be contacted by your physician at (314) 361–2371.

### 6. Birth Bonding: Bring on the 'Double Adam'!

1. See, *Birth and Bonding*, with the Instructor's Manual and Bibliography (Box 2092, Castro Valley, CA 94546: Media for Childbirth Education, 1977). See also M. H. Klaus and J. H. Kennell, *Parent-Infant Bonding* (St. Louis: C. V. Mosby Company, 1976, second edition). For the father's

role see D. McDonald, "Paternal Behavior at First Contact with the Newborn in a Birth Environment Without Intrusions," in *Birth Family Journal*, Fall 1978, pp. 123 ff.
2. Dr. Seuss, *How the Grinch Stole Christmas* (New York: Random House, 1957).

## 7. Parents and Children: For Each Other

1. C. S. Lewis, *The Lion, the Witch, and the Wardrobe* (New York: The Macmillan Company, 1950). The brief synopsis is summarized from pp. 75 ff.
2. Robert Sears' work is published under two major book titles, *Identification and Child Rearing* (Stanford: Stanford University Press, 1965), and *Patterns in Child Rearing* (New York: Harper and Row, 1957).
3. On "father absence," see E. Mavis Hetherington and Jan L. Deur, "The Effects of Father Absence on Child Development," *Young Children*, March 1971, pp. 233 ff.
4. For the effects of divorce, which almost always include the loss of the father's active presence, see also the frontier research of Thomas S. Parish at Kansas State University. He can furnish an extensive bibliography and reprints of his own published findings.
5. Dan Kiley, *The Peter Pan Syndrome* (New York: Dodd and Mead, 1983).
6. Kahlil Gibran, *The Prophet* (New York: Alfred Knopf, 1963) pp. 15–16.
7. For an excellent summary, see E. Mavis Hetherington and Jan L. Duer, "The Effects of Father Absence in Child Development," in *Young Children*, March 1971, pp. 233–245.

## 8. Adolescence: Is There Life After Puberty?

1. See my "Premature Puberty: Advice to Parents," *Christianity Today*, March 13, 1981, pp. 26 ff. I wrote and submitted the article under the title "Adolescence: Crucible for Creating Saints" as a dialogue with Dr. Ronald L. Koteskey's article submitted as "Adolescence: Unfortunate Creation of Western Society." His article was re-titled, "Growing Up Too Late, Too Soon." The contrast was therefore lost between his perspective that something has gone wrong, and mine that the pain of adolescence can evoke profound moral growth and sensitivity, hence, the "crucible for creating saints."
2. For a basic reading on "the secular trend," the tendency of each succeeding generation to reach pubescence earlier and to be taller than their parents, see Rolf E. Muuss, *Adolescent Behavior and Society: A Book of Readings* (New York: Random House, 1971). He authors the chapter, "Adolescent Development and the Secular Trend."
3. I first read of the connection between the pineal gland's production

of melatonin and the "secular trend" with its earlier development in *Psychology Today*, April 1975, when Gay Gaer Luce's article appeared: "Trust Your Body Rhythms," pp. 52 ff. Only later did I find her more extensive treatment in *Body Time* (Nashville: Parthenon, 1971, and the paperback reprint from New York: Bantam, 1973), especially pp. 270 ff., including the extensive bibliography on the pineal gland, beginning on p. 387. I was later to find a full "medical" drawing of how the light reaches the pineal gland, buried deep within the brain on humans, in the *New York Times* of June 23, 1981. There, Jane E. Brody detailed major findings about the pineal gland in an article, with drawings, "From Fertility to Mood, Sunlight Found to Affect Human Biology."

4. My information about the Dani tribe of New Guinea is based on conversations with Mike Maxey, one of my students who grew up among the Danis. He has given several hours of perspective, illustrated by movies and slides taken by his missionary family working alongside the anthropologist-missionary family which accompanied them in opening up Christian ministry among the Danis under the sponsorship of the Christian and Missionary Alliance.

5. The section, "Toward Freedom and Responsibility," is adapted from an article, "Six Ways to Handle Money and Kids," which first appeared in *Light and Life*, September 1973.

6. My use of "process system" for the female is pure invention. I was searching for a parallel descriptive phrase to Boyd McCandless' use of "hydraulic system" to describe the male. I studied with Dr. McCandless in the late 1960s, but he seems not to define "hydraulic system" in his several books on adolescence and sexual development, so I have tried to capture here what I found helpful in his course lectures.

7. Jesus' "rite of passage" in going to the Temple is recorded in Luke 2:41–52.

8. The Onan failure is recorded in Genesis 38.

9. See Sherman J. Silber, *The Male: From Infancy to Old Age, A Comprehensive and Clearly Written Guide to the Male Sexual System* (New York: Charles Scribner's Sons, 1981), "Erections During Sleep," pp. 14 ff.

### 9. Life, Love, and Eternity: The Ultimate Intimacy

1. See Dennis F. Kinlaw, "Charles Williams' Concept of Imaging Applied to 'The Song of Songs,'" in Wesleyan Theological Journal, Vol. 16, No. 1, Spring 1981, pp. 85–92.

2. Kinlaw, p. 90.

3. Kinlaw, p. 91.

4. I am indebted to one of my students, Janine Britt, for her extensive research into the biblical metaphors of divine-human bonding in the as yet unpublished essay linking human development findings with those biblical ideas. Her specific contribution here is the language "Hold Me Tight!" to denote the three-tiered cycle of birth-like bonding. I am re-

minded again of my oft-repeated assertion, "My students have taught me much more than I have taught them!"

5. Paul Tournier, *Secrets* (Richmond: John Knox Press, 1965).

6. C. S. Lewis, *The Great Divorce* (New York: The Macmillan Company, 1946). I have condensed here the essence of the exchange of pp. 16–24.

# Index

195